Making a Rapist

By

Luther Stidham

A former small town American police officer.

Edited by Mary Hoekstra

Revision 3

MoFo Book, LLC

Concord, NC

www.MoFoBooks.com

ATTENTION corporations, writing organizations, and writing conferences: Take 40% off and use this book as fundraisers, premiums, or gifts. Please contact the publisher:

MoFo Books, LLC

227 Laverne Dr. SW

Concord, NC 28025

(980) 255-0504

www.MoFoBooks.com

Library of Congress Control Number: 2016920251

Stidham, Luther

Making a Rapist / by Luther Stidham

p. cm

Includes Table of Content and Appendixes.

ISBN 978-0-9863902-4-1

10 9 8 7 6 5 4 3 2

Available Titles by Luther Stidham

*Falsely Accused Forever Branded*_____$24.95
260 page 6x9 Paperback

eBook Available_____$7.99

*DUI: How to Avoid Arrest!*_____$6.98
70 page 4x6 Paperback

eBook Available only on Amazon_____$2.99

*10 Best Slim Boosting Smoothies*_____$2.99
eBook Available only on Amazon

Dedication

Thanks to everyone who made this book possible—my family, particularly my wife, Danette, not only for putting up with the pace. But also for being so dedicated to getting me through my time of incarceration. Thanks to my three handsome boys, Jesse, Jordan, and Nathan, who provided plenty of support to keep this man sane?

Most of all, this book is dedicated to my friends and the gracious people of Boiling Spring Lakes, NC, whom I had the special honor of meeting and serving as a police officer.

And finally, I want to thank the countless people who know what it feels like when the law turns against you. We are living in a time when most suspects, in particularly people like myself—the poor—are treated as "guilty until proven innocent." We all know that's messed up and backwards; we're all guaranteed to be considered and treated as "innocent until proven guilty." The shame of it is, those of us who are branded "guilty" before a judge's gavel is ever raised up to start our trials, face pre-judgment, hypocrisy, and total disregard for our rights... and we face those things, and hear those things, from the "silver-tongued" devils who claim we are getting a fair trial.

Our nation's prisons are overflowing as a result of a judicial system in which the primary goals are conviction and collection, conviction of crime we did not commit and collection of money we do not have to give the devil his due. And that is a fair trial? Sure it is, if you set aside all of the Constitutionally defined and guaranteed rights of the defendant.

I hope you'll seize the opportunity to look into the legal system I'm describing. I hope you'll do what you can to change that terrible excuse for justice, because it is up to us to take a stand against corrupt judicial officials.

A prosecutor's misguided personal agenda should not be the guide for his or her obligation to ensure that both sides of the evidence are equally presented and equally weighed.

What you do with this opportunity is up to you? You can choose to do nothing but then nothing will ever change.

-Luther Stidham,
Eleven Seventy-Seven

Table of Contents

AUTHOR'S NOTE 13

PROLOGUE 16

CHAPTER 1 ....**19**

A FRESH START 19

BOILING SPRING LAKES, NC 23

BSL POLICE DEPARTMENT 24

QUALIFYING 25

CHAPTER 2 ....**29**

OFFICER GENE DAILEY 29

MOTIVATIONAL RESEARCH 33

BUDDY GYSEL.. 38

NOBODY RIDES FOR FREE... 39

BRITTANY LEWIS.. 41

BOBBY MCCORKLE 42

CHIEF RICHARD WHITE.. 47

THE POLICE ADMINISTRATOR 49

CHAPTER 3 ....**53**

YOU ARE THE CLOSEST THING TO PERFECT 53

CHIEF WHITE'S PRISONER 55

A DECEPTIVE KISS 61

A Falsified Ticket..62

CHAPTER 4..**69**

Multiple Unknown Injuries 69

CHAPTER 5..**79**

The Seduction Begins..79

CHAPTER 6..**83**

Suicide Kid 83

The Tender Voice of Old Mrs. Bailey.......................................88

CHAPTER 7..**95**

Planted Evidence..95

Can You See the Bruises 101

A Three-Way 104

A Broken Heart 105

CHAPTER 8..**109**

Chief, You're Under Arrest...109

CHAPTER 9..**115**

Alibi 115

CHAPTER 10..**119**

Log Back In 119

You'll Be Sorry 120

SINISTER E-MAILS 125

SINISTER TELEPHONE CALL 127

CHAPTER 11 .... **133**

SHADOW FIGURES 133

SPECIAL AGENT GHENT 136

INTERROGATION 141

SEARCH WARRANT 144

CHAPTER 12 .... **149**

BOND HEARING 149

CHAPTER 13 .... **151**

DRUG RAID 151

CHAPTER 14 .... **157**

MIKE RAMOS 157

PRIVATE INVESTIGATOR GENE HARDEE 162

CHAPTER 15 .... **167**

UNSPOKEN FORENSICS 167

CHAPTER 16 .... **173**

TRIAL DAY 173

CHAPTER 17 .... **183**

INNOCENT MEN GO TO PRISON EVERY DAY 183

CHAPTER 18 ....**189**

11:45 PM 189

MANUFACTURED FACTUAL BASIS 191

UNSIGNED BILL 193

CHAPTER 19 ....**195**

MY LAST NIGHT 195

CHAPTER 20 ....**199**

PIEDMONT CORRECTIONAL INSTITUTE 199

MODERN DAY SCARLET LETTER 205

NEARLY THERE 207

EPILOGUE **210**

APPENDIX A: **212**

ACTUAL CASE FILES AND REPORTS 212

DETECTIVE SIMPSON'S INCIDENT REPORT 215

AGENT GHENT'S AFFIDAVIT 217

DANIELLE SHRUGGS 221

SCOTT CISCO 223

JOHNNY T. LEWIS 225

DONNA MILLOWSKY 227

SBI DNA LABORATORY REPORT 230

CHIEF RICHARD WHITE..232

CLARA MILLINGS 234

BOBBY MCCORKLE...236

JEE L. HOLTON 238

SPECIAL AGENT GHENT'S SYNOPSIS..............................240

CONSPIRACY FAX 244

APPENDIX B:..**251**

THE AFTERMATH 251

ABOUT THE AUTHOR..**254**

AUTHOR'S NOTE

Making a Rapist is based on a true story drawn from a dozen interviews and hundreds of pages of documents. This title is the third revision of the memoir titled, *Falsely Accused Forever Branded.* In this revision, the previously altered names and personal descriptions of the people populating this story have been revealed because of their crimes. These criminals have been allowed to go free with their daily life while our State's Attorney General continues to ignore the severity of their crimes. My goal is to prompt plenty of publicity that will generate petitions to have both my case reviewed and criminal charges filed against the perpetrators.

The scenes described in this book were re-created, based on the information discovered within several video recording and documents, and from my own recollection of events that I have related to the best of my knowledge. I recognize that my memories of the events described in this book may differ from those of the people characterized here. This book is not intended to hurt or embarrass any of the individuals I portray. I'm sure each are fine, decent, and hard-working people who, in my opinion, made poor choices that ultimately led to my wrongful incarceration.

With a few exceptions, I have tried to keep the chronology as close to exact as I possibly could. In some instances, details and descriptions have been changed or recreated to coincide with the documentary record.

The dialogue has been re-created, based on the recollections of the participants and the actual case file documents.

In a sense my story is an exposé of a sinister ideology at work and is essential to public interest because of how it could affect the public's trust and opinion of our justice system.

Ask yourself these simple questions: What does the public expect from the criminal justice system? How does the public perceive various components of the criminal justice system? Is the system considered fair?

Finally, and most important: How much of public opinion is rooted in individual opinion, and in personal experiences?

You are the public; so am I.

I believe my personal story will reflect what factors currently affect public confidence and will reveal what has been learned about the way public confidence in the criminal justice system is built.

My story is a cut-away and cross section of a brutal, severely broken justice system. In the writing of this personal memoir, I have come to a level of understanding that makes it undeniably obvious that I am *not* alone. Others like me are mere trade-offs. We were bartered in exchange for a prosecutor's misguided, personal agenda.

I have come to another level of understanding that makes it undeniably clear that my story stands as a living example that *all* suspects are judicially presumed guilty until proven innocent, to one degree or another; and that all men are created equal, just not equally entitled to judicial protection by our laws, rules, and legal technicalities. The size of a man's bank account should not determine the quality of his defense options and prospects, nor the quality of his prosecutorial offense.

Like an investment, the judicial tag-team members brand their suspect through the media with a pre-trial guilty verdict as the payoff in the court of public opinion.

In my personal story, you are the jury.

While I have a surrogate doing the work for you, it is *you* who must ultimately sift through the information, and it is you who will be left thunderstruck and boiling with rage by what you discover.

PROLOGUE

SBI Exposed For Concealing Illegal Images

Suppose it was discovered that you produced and stored images of child pornography on our computer. Now suppose both the FBI and NC SBI were aware then seized that computer. What are the chances that you would be charged with Possession of Child Pornography?

State and Federal law prohibits the production, distribution, reception, and possession of an image of child pornography. There are no exceptions to these laws. Therefore, not one person would be excluded from these laws, right?

Wrong, not unless you are one of NC State Bureau of Investigation's alleged victim.

So what did the SBI do after discovering pornographic images of their 14-year-old alleged victim stored on the family computer?

"They scan it for other illegal images then used forensic software to destroy the evidence," Luther Stidham, a former police officer for the town of Boiling Spring Lakes, North Carolina said.

On September 11, 2006, North Carolina State Bureau of Investigation Special Agent Charles L. Ghent interviewed B. Lewis, a 14-years old female in an alleged Statutory Rape case. Ghent, never expecting his recorded interview to fall into the hands of Luther Stidham, told Lewis and her family that he had found "some potentially embarrassing stuff" on their home computer. A computer that Lewis, her father and brother all shared.

Ghent went on to add what other images he found. "Not just yours but what other people in the family might have been looking at that, you know, might get paranoid if exposed." Ghent then added. "The point is we're going to have to go back through and look. We have some stuff that can hopefully dig deeper in there and pull some things up."

In a move that would suggest Ghent was more concerned with protecting the Lewis family from a federal conviction, what Ghent does next is both soul shocking and illegal:

"We have some other methods that we can go back in and delete stuff," Ghent added.

A true story of corruption, abuse of justice and deception set in Brunswick County, North Carolina. *Making a Rapist,* involves a double-dealing SBI agent and a documented, narcissistic, suicidal juvenile who seeks revenge on those who oppose her.

SBI Special Agent Ghent never lost his poise. A master craftsman of his trade, he never showed a trace of emotion. He was the underdog that stockpiled fear in his suspect with a mixture of wicked interpretations and unscientific experiments precisely calculated to produce the result he sought. If Ghent was out to make an arrest, he stalked his prey like a wooded animal. He was an expert at setting traps and manipulating his victim's path. No officer dared to confront him, for fear of retaliation.

CHAPTER 1

A FRESH START

As far back as I can remember, even when I was a little boy, I looked forward to vacation time more than I looked forward to Christmas. Don't get me wrong; Christmas time was great; I always asked Santa to bring me "cop stuff."

I asked for "cop stuff" because I wanted to be a policeman when I grew up, but vacation time meant one thing better than Christmas: a week of sun and fun in the sand.

For one week every year, my parents would take my siblings and me to Oak Island, North Carolina. That long drive down Highway 211 was one of the most exciting parts of the trip for me. My mother would always say, "We're on 211 now," and I knew what that meant. I would get goose bumps and that butterfly-in-my stomach feeling. I would giggle with excitement as I looked out the window. My legs were just long enough that my little feet swung carelessly over the edge of the back seat. When I was a child, I wanted so badly to live at the beach.

Just after my 18th birthday, in late December 1989, I was already married and had my first son, Jesse. Two years later, my second son, Jordan, was born. I wasn't the greatest husband, nor was I that good at holding down steady employment. I was simply too young, just too immature, for either responsibility. My wife, Jen, grew tired of my irresponsibility so we drifted apart.

A couple of years after Jordan was born, I took a job as a restaurant manager in North Myrtle Beach, South Carolina. I moved my family to the beach in hopes of rekindling a long-burned out flame and get my marriage back in order.

It didn't work.

It wasn't long before I contacted one of my best friends, Brad Kerley, and asked him to move down to Myrtle Beach. I was just bored to death and so alone that I needed a friend around to keep my spirits up.

I hired Brad, as my assistant manager at the restaurant and the two of us became after-hour party animals in our own restaurant. We held pizza dough and ice fights nearly every night. Not to mention eating endless pizza.

On one of my nights off, Brad was closing. He had told me he hired a new girl, so I headed to the restaurant to check her out. As I pulled up, I saw this beautiful blonde vacuuming the carpet near the front door. I walked in and as soon as I looked her way, her hazel eyes captivated me. I smiled and then she smiled back. I made up an excuse to help Brad close the place down, just so I could get to know her.

We began talking more and more when we worked together, so I finally made sure her schedule matched mine. I spent more time watching her than paying attention to my own job. Within a few weeks, I felt alive again. There was only one problem though; I was still married.

Despite my vows to Jen, I had fallen in love with the new girl, Danette. We had our first kiss in the back of the restaurant. She was cutting up vegetables for the salad bar and I had built up the courage to just walk up and plant one on her beautiful lips. She acted as if she was a bit thrown off by my boldness, but her smile said otherwise.

Danette and I both knew that it was wrong for us to have feelings for each other and for me to still be married. Danette thought it would be best if she moved back to Charlotte on her own, while I stayed at the beach. We even stopped communicating, but I never stopped wanting to be with her.

A few months later, Jen and I agreed to separate, and soon afterwards I moved back to Charlotte. Jen moved our two boys to her mother's home in Mt. Holly, North Carolina.

Danette and I picked up our relationship again, and by 1996, we had given birth to our son, Nathan. Danette and I married nine years later at the Chapel by the Sea in Myrtle Beach. Over the next six years, I grew up a lot, but still bounced around from job to job, always looking for what fit me the best. There were two things that I never stopped wanting, though: to live at the beach and to become a police officer.

It was the spring of 2003 when my brother, Dennis moved to the beach. Within the next year he had talked my mother and me into moving there, as well. We all sat down and developed a plan to launch a family owned fencing business.

I made big plans for my wife and son. All I ever wanted to do was provide for my family. It was going to be a new beginning for us. Danette and I were very much in love, which made waking up together that much sweeter. I thought I had every detail of our new beginning worked out.

My family's fencing business grew quickly through the summer of 2004, until my brother and I had a disagreement that nearly led to a fistfight. I decided it would be best for our relationship if I left the family business, so I took a mechanic's position at Yaupon Service Center.

Meanwhile, I had stumbled across an ad for a police officer's position in the *Stateport Pilot* newspaper. I contacted the Oak Island Police Department but, to my great disappointment, learned that I had to pass a Basic Law Enforcement Training course on my own. Besides accomplishing that, in order for me to enroll, I needed a sponsor from a local police department. So after a few get acquainted ride-along with some of the officers from Boiling Spring Lakes, I was able to convince their chief, Richard White, to sponsor me through rookie school.

Fortunately, Mark and James Warren, the owners of Yaupon Service Center, not only encouraged me, but also allowed me to maintain my employment as a mechanic while attending the police academy at Brunswick Community College. It was the longest six months of my life, but somehow, I graduated. I'll never forget how generous the Warren brothers were. They are the two most generous men that I have ever come to know.

BOILING SPRING LAKES, NC

Boiling Spring Lakes is the third-largest town in Brunswick County, North Carolina. It consists mostly of wildlife preservation areas. "BSL" is what the locals call their town, and it gets its name from a large, underground spring. The force of the spring makes the water appear to be boiling when it reaches the surface. The water comes straight up from the earth, exiting through a hole nearly 10 feet wide. The spring pumps out about one million gallons of water every day.

As the story goes, during the 1800s the indigenous Indians who lived in the area would stop to drink from the spring when they traveled back to their homes from their coastal fishing treks. For many years, there was a large log caught in the current, so the Indians called it "Bouncing Log Spring."

"Bouncing Log Spring," is tucked away about 50 yards off Cherokee Road in a heavily wooded area. Some of the locals in BSL's history tried to encase the powerful, watery beast with a circular brick wall. The restriction of the wall forced the spring to open the earth up again, just a few feet outside its encasement. The ground shook violently and, as if the beast had a mind of its own, it slowly picked away at the wall and returned to its original home.

Sinkholes are a frequent occurrence in BSL, and those are what formed most of its 50 lakes. The largest lake in BSL is referred to as "Big Lake." Several small ponds formed Big Lake. An early settler to BSL finished the lake's construction by cutting down trees and building a dam on the far north end. A large sinkhole opened up beneath its surface, and Big Lake began draining like a small whirlpool. Once the water level dropped low enough, the town packed the hole with clay, all the while hoping that would patch the problem. Years later, Big Lake still hasn't recovered to its full potential.

BSL POLICE DEPARTMENT

The old City Hall and the Police Department shared a former ranch-style brick house. It reminded me of a small country setting with the feeling of home. The ladies working in the City Hall were always kind and pleasant to speak with. The Police Department was the smaller of the two organizations and consisted of three rooms: the chief's office, the lieutenant's offices, and the front lobby. Each space accommodated six officers.

The City Hall was connected to the PD offices by a hallway and held the kitchen, Water and Inspection Departments, evidence room, bathrooms, and the city manager's office. There once had been a plush couch kept in Lt. Ledbetter's office until Officer Gene Dailey repeatedly got caught sleeping when he was on duty.

"Get that damn couch out of here!" Chief Richard White shouted, as the story goes.

The people of BSL were exceedingly warm, gracious, and polite. Their little town had a beautiful golf course, three gas stations, two traffic lights, one automotive repair shop, a middle school, a high school, and among other things, a Dollar General store.

QUALIFYING

After I graduated from the police academy, I immediately started filling out applications at all the local police departments in the surrounding area. After learning that most of my rookie classmates had already been hired as police officers, I immediately got worried. I had a misdemeanor criminal record (traffic stuff) from back in 1989 and I thought it had come back to haunt me. On May 2, 2005, I had abandoned all hope of becoming a police officer and was at work at the Yaupon Service Center. I had just finished lunch one day when my cell phone rang.

"This is Chief Richard White with the Boiling Spring Lakes Police Department. Are you still looking for an officer's position?"

"Heck yeah." I replied almost yelling.

"Be here in the morning, say 10 o' clock," he said, laughing at my enthusiasm.

By 9:45 a.m. the following morning, I reported to the PD. The chief and I drove to the Brunswick County Gun Range where I had to qualify in handgun and shotgun proficiency with at least an 85 percent accuracy rate. Having shot over 1,500 rounds with the Glock 9mm in rookie school; I had qualified in the low 90th percentile. I was comfortable with my 9mm, but my confidence quickly disintegrated when I was informed the BSL Police Department used a Glock 45.

"Do I get any practice shots?" I asked.

The chief responded, "Why? You know how to shoot, right?"

"Of course, but I need to get a feel for this handgun," I replied.

"Go ahead," Chief White said. "Take one or two shots then."

I was never good at following orders with any precision. I just listened to the chief's version of "practice shots," and followed my own version of "two or three practice shots." I emptied the magazine as quickly as I could pull the trigger.

The chief put his hands on his hips and said, "I said one or two, not the whole damn magazine." I smiled at him with a devious look. The chief walked to the target and then said, "You still have to qualify at night, so..." He paused a few seconds, then he said, "It looks dark to me. How about you?"

It was only about 11 am, but I replied without hesitation, "It looks dark to me." The chief walked down the firing line about three targets away, which made me very nervous.

"Are you okay there?" I asked.

"If you shoot me all the way over here, you're fired," he replied.

I swapped out magazines and unloaded 13 more rounds from the Glock 45. After a quick calculation of my pattern, the chief asked, "You think you're hot shit now, don't you?"

"Why do you say that? What'd you qualify at?" I asked.

The chief just smiled again. I gathered from his expression, between the two of us, I was the better shot.

All the application process had been completed. I was eager to be sworn in. On that day, Chief White held a Bible in one hand and the oath of the PD in his other, then he said, "Place your left hand on the Bible, and raise your right hand. Read from this."

The room was packed with some of the town's commissioners and the mayor. Damn, I was so nervous, but it sure looked like my lifelong wish had come true.

I have always been one of those people who really enjoy helping others. No matter who or what they needed, I've always tried to be there, to lend a hand. To me, the day I was sworn in as a police officer was the first day of the rest of my life. I had made it. I could finally provide for my wife and son. I had fulfilled both of my childhood dreams – to be a policeman and to live near the beach.

Unfortunately, my worst nightmare began taking shape quickly and immediately. It became undeniably clear to me that when it came to the BSL PD, I didn't belong.

I did earn the respect of many of the citizens in BSL. Most of the folks had previously just surrendered to the authority-abusing officers of my police department. I believe my altruistic personality showed me to be a different type of cop, so I became well known throughout town. On numerous occasions, the locals specifically requested me to be their transporting officer, or requested me to come to an accident scene, or an incident, and take their reports. That meant a lot to me; it meant the folks thought I was doing a good job. They came to see they could trust me, and see I treated them the same way they treated me, with respect.

Oblivious to the harassment I would receive as an officer later, the people of BSL seemed to enjoy feeding me on my lunch breaks. I enjoyed eating, so that arrangement worked great. I accepted their friendly meals, so they continued to offer me their friendly meals. Of course, my newfound respect, my new mutual friendships, and folks feeding me regularly, made Chief White and Officer Dailey jealous. Most of the time they accused me of engaging in some form of infidelity, as though I was being unfaithful to… what?

Oh, yeah… unfaithful to their way of doing business and public relations in the town.

CHAPTER 2

OFFICER GENE DAILEY

Officer Gene Dailey, a six-foot tall, blue-eyed man with salt-and-pepper hair, often complained that I was not stern enough to be a BSL cop. It didn't take long before I was questioning whether Officer Dailey was a barbaric man. I found out one of the sources of his vengeful attitude. When he was on duty one day, Dailey told me, he had driven home unexpectedly. He walked into his home, only to find his wife in bed with another man, a man who had been a friend of both of ours.

The way he told the story to me, Dailey apparently went into an immediate, vicious rage. He told me he punched holes in the walls, and busted up a wide screen television. Later, his wife told me that at the time, she thought having sex in their bed, with one of her husband's friends, was allowed. She looked at it like she got a "free pass" to do that because she had treated Dailey to sexual threesomes a few times. When Dailey was in the company of other people, he often went into details about his wife's bisexuality. He'd say things like, "She's a carpet muncher."

With MySpace® expanding, I started my own profile. I uploaded pictures of my patrol vehicle, the police department, and my wife and family. Right away I received several friend requests from both males and females, most of them BSL locals, or from nearby Southport, Oak Island and Wilmington. Dailey's sister, a pretty mid-twenty something, requested to be included in my friends list on MySpace. I had never met her. Hell, I didn't even know Dailey had a sister until then. I agreed to her request, but not too long after that, during one of Dailey's and my squabbling moments, I made sure Dailey saw her picture on my home page. He reacted like I thought he would.

"How do you know my sister?" he asked.

"A gentleman never tells," I said with a smile. And just as I expected, his already-irked demeanor got hotter.

A short time after that revelation about his sister, Dailey found out that his wife had confided in me about their separation. That upset him immensely, and from that moment on, he dogged me with extremely malicious intent. Dailey believed that I had "bumped uglies" with his wife and with his sister at some point.

Faced with Dailey's suspicions, and knowing he believed he was right to be suspicious, I just said, "So what if we did?"

I made a point to remind Dailey it was his own guilty conscious speaking for itself. I added fuel to that fire by saying, "You left your wife on Mother's Day."

His face turned red, and I added, "So what's it to you?"

•

I have never admitted, nor denied, Dailey's accusations, and I never will. I've kept the truth about what he accused me of to myself, close to the vest, because of how Dailey treated me and how he treated everyone else in BSL. Even today, as I write this book, I get immense amusement at the thought of Dailey wondering, but never knowing for the rest of his life, whether I ever tasted his sister and his wife. Hell, maybe I did sample the two ladies, and maybe both of them at the same time.

But maybe I didn't. I'll never tell.

•

A few weeks later, one of the guys from the BSL volunteer fire department invited me to dinner. Dailey was already steamed, so on one of his more jealous days, he confronted me and asked, "How do you get invited to dinner so much, Mother Teresa?"

"Mother Teresa" was a nickname Dailey had picked out for me because of my personality.

The chief, laughing at Dailey's gesture asked, "Is he letting you bang his wife or something?" I tried to ignore their childish questions, but then the chief said, "Nobody else has ever been called on or invited as much as you."

I looked up from my paperwork as the chief continued, "What the hell are you doing out there?"

I was pretty damned insulted by then, so I fired back, "I'm just a nice guy. You should try it sometime, assholes!"

I wasn't sure whether I had returned the insult, or even the same sarcastic humor, but it just felt good to say it anyway.

Officer Dailey replied, "Oh bullshit! Nice guy my ass. You're fucking his wife." I just shook my head in disgust and went back to my paperwork.

I often got the impression that they wished I *was* messing with Dailey's or someone else's wife, just so they could use it against me. The BSL Police Department had a reputation for employing officers who often abused their authority or used their badges as sex passes.

Don't get me wrong, there were a few good officers there at one time, but that didn't last long after Richard White took over as chief. One of the town's officers had been killed in the line of duty and the others eventually moved on to other departments.

As a police officer, I was more than fair. I was honest, helpful, and tactful when it came to upholding my duties. I never would sweat the small stuff. And why should I? There were always bigger fish to fry, like domestic violence, for example. That was my pet peeve. And I admit, I sometimes dealt with the women-beaters severely, just so I could give them a "teachable moment," a brief opportunity to learn.

MOTIVATIONAL RESEARCH

Just a week or two after my little heart-warming exchange with Dailey and the chief, I went on patrol on my own. I was called out to a domestic violence incident. When I arrived, an intoxicated man, about six feet tall, with dark hair, had beaten up his girlfriend. Her daughter, whom I'll call Abby, had seen the whole thing. I learned that Abby jumped on this man's back while he had her mother pinned on the ground. He flung her to the floor as well. Abby was just nine years old.

This man, Tim, thought he could bully a five-foot seven-inch tall cop, so when I arrived he approached me in an aggressive manner.

"One more step and I'll knock your ass out." I said.

Abby took refuge behind me and then she grabbed my hand.

"You have her scared to death." I then added.

I looked down at Abby trying to figure out what to say without scaring her. I said, "Congratulations, you got the wrong one today."

I walked Abby across the room to her mother. I held Abby's hand in one hand and reached down with my other to help Cary, her mother, get up off the floor. Cary's eyes were swollen and her nose and lips were bloody. She moved to the couch and sat down, with Abby on her lap. I stood between Tim and the couch.

"Does that make you feel like a man?" I asked him.

The anger began raging inside me. I reached around my utility belt and unlocked my handcuffs. I gripped the cuffs so tightly in my hand that my knuckles turned white.

"Turn around. Put your hands behind your back. You're under arrest," I said, trying to remain professional for Abby's sake, but still hoping Tim wanted to fight.

"You and what army?" Tim asked.

Now that was exactly the response I had hoped for. "I *wish* you would give me a reason." I replied.

By that point, I was supposed to have called for back up. And I did; I just waited a bit longer.

"Turn around or I will turn you around." I said, and then made a sarcastic gesture by sucking my teeth. I hoped to entice Tim into a fight.

To my disappointment, Tim turned around and placed his hands behind his back. I bent his thumbs back pretty hard, hoping to make him swing at me. Unfortunately, he didn't. Once I locked him in the cuffs, I escorted him outside to the porch and forced him to sit down. Then I called for back up.

"Seventy-seven to seven-five?" I asked.

"Go ahead Luke," Dailey replied.

"Need assistance with a domestic. Non-emergency."

While I waited for Dailey, I stood post in the doorway so I could keep an eye on Tim and speak with Cary and Abby at the same time. As I took notes, Cary stopped speaking right in the middle of a sentence. Then Abby screamed and pointed behind me. The hairs on my neck stood up. Before I knew it, I swung an elbow behind me. It was Tim, of course. He thought he would sneak up on me. The punch only stunned him for a second, but that was long enough for me to wrap my arms around his broad chest. I swept my foot behind him and then flung him to the deck hard. As I knelt over him, I asked, "What did you think you were doing, Tim?"

Officer Dailey pulled up and then ran up to the porch. He and I locked Tim in the back of my patrol car. I finished my report with Cary, and then Abby reminded me why I had chosen to be a police officer. She grabbed my hand again and followed me to the edge of the porch. She tapped me on the arm asking, "Police man?"

I looked down as she wiped tears from her cheeks.

"Please don't let him come back here, okay?" she said, tears still running down her rosy red cheeks.

It seemed like she just couldn't wipe them away fast enough. Abby then reached out both arms. I knelt down on one knee, and she hugged me for what seemed like forever. Feeling like I had a softball in my throat, I replied, "I won't, Abby."

I was determined to keep my word with Abby, but on the trip to jail Tim got out of his seatbelt. He kept yelling in my ear as I was driving, "You stupid son-of-a-bitch."

I turned my rear view mirror so I could keep an eye on him. We made it to an area of Highway 87 where numerous deer crossed the road. By this time, Tim had leaned back in his seat and was making a snorting sound. I looked back to see he was about to spit on me. I waited, and when he thrust himself forward, I slammed on the brakes.

Smack!

I knew that wire cage would come in handy someday. Tim's face slammed into it hard. He fell back in the back seat and then shouted, "That hurt!" He leaned up and asked, "You meant to do that, didn't you?"

"Bet that hurt like hell, didn't it?" I asked. A smile of satisfaction spread across my face as I kicked the throttle to the floor. I jammed on the brakes and then kicked the throttle a few more times. I finally just nailed the throttle to the floor. I may have even jerked the wheel back and forth some. For some reason, Tim sure did roll around like a loose basketball in my backseat.

Like to beat on women do you? I thought.

I guess I hit about 115 miles-per-hour before I slammed on the brakes again. The tires squealed for a really long time. I hit a soft shoulder and slid off the road. My car spun wildly in circles into a field just off Danwood Road. Weeds and sticks slapped the side of my vehicle in protest to my reckless driving.

"You crazy motherfucker!" Tim screamed as we came to rest.

Plumes of dust and smoke rolled up the side of his door as Tim asked, "What are you doing?"

I took a quick survey of our orientation to the road and heard Tim squirming around and mumbling, "You're crazy man!"

I grabbed the steering wheel tightly, and as I stared over the hood, I asked him, "Are you scared?"

"Yeah, I'm scared to death, man," Tim replied. "Are you trying to kill me?"

I jumped out of the car, flung open the back door, and leaped in on Tim.

"Now you know what it feels like to be at someone else's mercy!" I screamed in his face. Tim curled up in the corner of the back seat.

"Are ... We ... Clear?" I shouted.

Tim's face went blank. I ripped my sidearm from its holster and pinned his head against the window with the tip of the barrel. "ARE ... WE ... CLEAR?" I repeated, this second time shouting with vicious fury.

"Yes sir! Yes sir!" he said. "Please, man!"

I crawled back out and then drove through the field making my way back to the road. Tim, still curled up in the back, never spoke another word.

We arrived at the jail and I pulled into the sally port. I waited for the gate to close behind me and then locked my sidearm in the trunk. I opened the back door for Tim, and that's when I noticed... Clearly, he did get my point.

"Well now, isn't that cute? The big bad woman-beater pissed his pants." I grabbed his arm to pull him out of the back seat and said, "You tinker bell sissy. Get out of my damn car."

●

I have long since realized that some people on one end of the spectrum may call what I did to Tim "police brutality," but then I asked myself, "What would the thousands of battered women have called it? ... An eye-for-an-eye maybe?"

And that's when I decided the sub-chapter heading, "Motivational Research," fit quite nicely. And ... I offer no apologies for my actions.

This one's for you, Abby.

BUDDY GYSEL

I met Buddy Gysel at a community festival shortly after I was hired at the BSL PD. Buddy was a 20-year-old BSL volunteer firefighter. Raised in Philadelphia, Buddy and his family moved to BSL when he was 15-years-old. He was tall and had dark brown hair, but he was not a very attractive individual. There were several untreated acne scars on his face. Buddy was, however, hilarious and entertaining. What his looks lacked, his personality more than made up for. He and I quickly became good friends.

I was on duty during a town festival and had been elected to assist during the event by giving rides in my patrol vehicle. Buddy introduced himself and invited me to the fire department's cookout later that evening. I had already made plans for dinner but I thought it would be a good opportunity for me to introduce myself to the BSL VFD.

"If I don't get busy, I'll drop in." I replied. Just then, I remembered a brief conversation I had earlier with Dailey. So, I asked Buddy, "Nobody's going to get mad or anything are they?"

"Maybe the other police will, but not us," Buddy replied.

Buddy told me that he wanted me to meet a girl by the name of Brittany Lewis; he had met her in church during a youth dance and cookout. Brittany was dating Bobby McCorkle at the time, but apparently that didn't deter her or Buddy from social experimenting.

NOBODY RIDES FOR FREE

I hadn't even completed my second month on patrol when I got another invitation to one of the BSL VFD's weekly dinner meetings. On that evening, I was off duty and decided to take Buddy up on his offer. Buddy was to be promoted to sergeant that night. He was decked out in his navy blue dress uniform with a variety of Honor Guard medals and medallions. Several of his friends and family members attended that evening, too. The VFD dinner meetings became nearly a community-wide event, so this particular meal and gathering made the acknowledgment of his achievements even better. It was no secret to anyone that BSL police officers never felt it necessary to attend VFD functions. My attendance made me the oddball with the other police officers.

The meeting room was filled with table after table of food and drinks. The variety seemed endless. In the far corner sat four of the town's best gossips. The fire chief, Ed Anderson, was laughing at his lieutenant's comical impression of Chief White. Nearly 40 people were spread out in groups among the tables. Ten here, 15 there, some standing, some still eating, but nevertheless, all were catching up on the latest rumors.

Buddy and I sat talking for a while and then he filled me in on his relationship with his ex-girlfriend, Brittany Lewis. Buddy said, "Brittany is so fascinated with you. You're all she talks about."

I was a bit taken aback by his statement. I didn't remember meeting anyone by that name. Buddy, in one of his comic moments, raised his voice several octaves, mocking Brittany's squeaky voice. He tied his shirt in a knot on his side and then jerked his head around.

"Have you seen Officer Stidham today?" He asked with his falsetto tone.

He pretended to smoke a cigarette, too, as though he was a high-class schmuck. I just rolled about, laughing so hard at his impression.

BRITTANY LEWIS

Brittany was a young female who had the look of an innocent child. She grew up around the BSL area. Her mother and father had split up when she was 11. Sherri, her mother, had apparently walked in on Brittany's father while he was having sex with one of her friends. Brittany had been hiding in her mother's closet and smoking a cigarette when her father, Johnny, brought his girlfriend home for a quickie. Brittany sat watching the whole event unfold through the cracks of the closet doors.

By the time Brittany had turned 12, she had already run away from home three times and was almost a full-blown alcoholic. Her wrists were scarred where she had been cutting herself with steak knives and razor blades. Brittany never really had the nerve to cut too deeply. Her parents overlooked her smoking since they could never make her stop. Even at such a young age, Brittany learned how to manipulate people by watching her mother bring home a different trick every night.

After her divorce, Sherri became a prostitute. She never had to work before her divorce but the financial support was gone and Johnny never paid child support. Sherri just returned to what she knew best: drugs, alcohol, and prostitution.

Brittany sometimes took her digital camera and hid in her mother's closet; she'd record men having sex with her mother. She often turned the camera on her girlfriends and herself when they pretended to perform to an imaginative audience.

BOBBY MCCORKLE

I got better acquainted with Brittany's background during patrol a few weeks after the VFD dinner and Buddy's promotion. I was on routine patrol near the outskirts of Boiling Spring Lakes. It was getting dark outside and I was the only officer on duty when my police radio came alive, "C-COM, eleven seventy-seven?"

●

C-COM was police jargon for Central Communications, the 911-dispatch center in Brunswick County.

●

"Eleven seventy-seven, go ahead." I replied.

Dispatch told me they'd just received a call for officer's assistance to take a stalking report.

"Ten-four. Send address to my pager. Show me en route." I replied.

Moments later, my pager displayed the caller's address:

```
Caller-Bobby McCorkle
Address-10142 E. Boiling Spring Rd.
        Caller stated being stalked by ex-
        girlfriend; stated is being accused of
        assault.
```

·

Three main roads in a triangular shape encase Boiling Spring Lakes, so that made driving to any location simple. Highway 133 runs from the tip of the triangle north to south. Also known as Highway 87, George II Highway runs southeast to northwest, forming the bottom of the triangle. East Boiling Springs Road connects the two. Several side streets run like spaghetti inside the triangle and connect to all sides. Traveling from the farthest point to the opposite farthest point took about 30 minutes.

·

I arrived at the address and pulled into the driveway, I had already made it a habit to leave my patrol vehicle running with the headlights on and pointing directly at the house - a must-do for the night shift. I checked in with dispatch,

"C-COM, eleven seventy-seven? Show me on scene."

Bobby McCorkle was a 16-year-old teenager who was about five-feet, six-inches tall, with brown hair. He had just received his driver's license a few months prior. As I started toward the house, I noticed a black Buick Regal SS in the driveway.

I walked up the concrete steps to the front door and gave a firm knock on the door. "Police department," I said with an authoritative voice.

Bobby, a stocky football star, opened the door and told me, "I'm the one who called you."

"Tell me what's going on," I responded, and took out my notepad and pen.

I followed Bobby into the foyer while he described his situation. "I broke up with my girlfriend last week because I found out she had been cheating on me with this guy named Buddy," he said.

I asked Bobby his age, and he told me that he was 16.

I asked, "What is the name and age of your ex-girlfriend?"

"Her name is, Brittany Lewis," Bobby said. "She lives on Juniper."

I noticed right away that he had dodged the last part of my question. So I asked a second time, "How old is she?" Bobby appeared to get nervous and looked down at the floor.

As I asked a third time, I mimicked sign language, "How ... old ... is ... she?" "Thirteen."

"Okay, tell me what happened," I said.

"Brittany is all upset and now she is threatening to call the police and say that I beat her up. Brittany is the type that will do that. She will even hit herself until she gets bruises and say I done it. I recorded her accusing a friend of mine named Brad of trying to rape her. He got into a lot of trouble over that."

Moments later, his telephone rang. Bobby looked at the caller ID before he picked it up. He showed the screen to me and said, "Officer? That's her calling."

I told him to just answer the call like normal, and if she made any threats to just hand me the phone.

Bobby's mother, Jan, picked up the telephone instead.

"Brittany? The police's here. Stop calling my house and my son," she said, and then she slammed the telephone down.

I had a duty to fulfill, so I had to ask, "Bobby ... Did you hit her?"

"No sir, I did not," he replied.

There wasn't much I could do at that point, so I told Bobby and his mom that I would fill out the report later. Just before I left I said, "If you want a copy, stop by the police department tomorrow. If this Brittany calls about any assault, I'll contact you. But I'll still have to do a report. Meanwhile, let's talk about the black Buick in the driveway."

Jan had returned to her kitchen, but when she heard me speak about the Buick, she stomped back into the foyer.

She asked Bobby, "What have you done?"

"Nothing, Mom," Bobby replied.

I recognized his Buick. We had received several calls about that car racing up and down the road. I told Bobby, "If I catch you ... and I will, I will issue you a citation. Are we clear?"

"Yes sir," he replied.

Jan interrupted, "He'll not be driving for a while. I promise you that."

Back at the police department, I looked up Bobby McCorkle and Brittany Lewis in the database. Bobby's name was searched first but returned no results. Brittany Lewis's name, however, returned a few reports as far back as January 2004.

She had two runaway reports, and two reports of attempted rape, by a parent and by her older brother, Brad. The State had filed charges against her father, Johnny T. Lewis. The prosecutor had dismissed the case after the third day. Brad was placed on house arrest during his investigation. His charges were later dismissed, too.

One note in her file read:

> Victim recanted her statement. Stated she only
> made the rape allegation up because she was mad
> at her father. Johnny, her father, stated he
> does not wish to file charges. History shows
> mental incompetence.
>
> Judge Ola Lewis recommended dismissal. DSS
> contacted. No further action needed.

I filed the report about the Bobby McCorkle incident along with the other reports about Brittany. A review of the previous history revealed a follow-up would only be dismissed. Besides that, the fact that Brittany shared the same last name as Brunswick County's most distinguished judge, who also lived in BSL, struck me as a little too coincidental.

CHIEF RICHARD WHITE

The problems that led to my legal tribulations actually began about three weeks or so after I was hired at the BSL PD. In my time as a BSL law enforcement officer, I witnessed corruption, lies, massive adultery, and multiple law violations, all related in some way to that department. Even more tragic than that, I worked around the offenders. They were my supervisors, shift partners, and field-training officers. Don't get me wrong, I was no angel either, but nothing I did compared to what those guys did.

The chief, for example, was a tall slender man in his early 60s. He was bald and had a grin that just looked evil. In my opinion, his actions conveyed the message that he was sneaky and underhanded. Eventually, his presence acted on me like a stinging, hot irritant.

The chief drove a white, un-marked Ford Crown Vic. One day in the early summer of 2005, I was patrolling near the outskirts of BSL again, and came to an abandoned parking lot. There was a dirt road leading off the backside of that parking lot. The road ran into a wooded area that hid a small pond. There were several bushes that covered up where the pavement ended and the dirt road began. The parking lot had been abandoned for so long that grass, bushes, and small trees had broken open and had grown through the pavement. Some of the trees had grown to be over five and six feet tall. The other officers and I would use the trees and bushes as camouflage.

Turning into the parking lot, I could see the back end of a white car just barely sticking out from behind the bushes.

What's going on back there? I wondered expecting to find someone engaged in mischief.

I rolled up on the car very slowly, and as I got within feet of the car, I recognized it. It was the chief in his Crown Vic. I quickly hit the brakes and then put it in reverse. I tried to roll out the same way I came in ... very slowly. I must've made some noise, because suddenly the chief turned to look over his left shoulder.

I noticed a lot of squirming around in his vehicle so I stopped, and that's when I watched the chief lean back. I got the impression he was zipping up his pants. To my surprise, a woman's head and shoulders and torso rose up from Chief's lap, which strengthened my perception even further.

"Oh shit! The chief's getting a hummer," I said, laughing. "Wait till I tell Dailey."

I recognized Chief's lady friend as Amy Armstrong. I identified her to be Chief White's special friend, and to be about the same age as he. I could have been wrong, but that was my opinion, based on what I had just witnessed. She was a nurse's assistant at a nearby urgent care center. Amy peeked across the seat scanning the area.

You dirty old fart. I thought as I pulled away.

THE POLICE ADMINISTRATOR

Not long after that glimpse into Chief White's preferences, I was promoted to the traffic officer's position associated with the Governor's Highway Safety Program. Actually, nobody wanted the position because the chief had to approve the disbursement of the funds. I only found out *after* I took the position that the chief pushed the envelope with misappropriation of the funds.

Shortly after my promotion, the chief hired *himself* a police administrator. Her name was Allison. She was susceptible to believing just about anything. She was married, with a daughter, and originally from Ontario, Canada. Allison and her daughter moved to BSL to attend to family issues while her husband stayed behind.

Allison was in her early 40s, anorexic and tall. She had no police training or certifications. Chief White decided to promote her to the director's position over the National Crime Information Center in the BSL Police Department. I was the only officer in BSL to be trained and certified with the NCIC database system, so Allison's promotion didn't go over very well with me. I felt that it had been my certification that had earned the PD its terminal, not whatever was lurking between Allison's legs. Chief White decided to make me give Allison my user-name and password. As if that wasn't bad enough, then the chief wanted me to teach her how to use the system.

Any NCIC-authorized user can attest that it was strictly forbidden to give out your user-name and password, so I told the chief, "You have to be certified by the Department of Justice. You know that."

The chief responded, "I'm going to certify her. Go ahead and give her your password. She'll issue you new ones."

That hit me hard. I didn't like the fact that the chief was trying to make me break the rules. That was a serious offense, but he was my boss, so I asked, "Is that an order?"

He nodded his head yes, and I had to accept the fact that I could only buck him and his orders so far, and no farther. I told him, "You can't just certify her, and she has to be trained. If they find out, it's your ass not mine."

I wrote down my information on a sticky note. I threw it into the trashcan as I walked out of the building. As I left, I said, "What you do with this after I leave is your business, but I can't train her."

For days, I monitored Allison's access to the NCIC system with my login information. The system kept a detailed activity log, and the Department of Justice regularly kept tabs on who was doing what.

"You can't just run random tags." I said. "There has to be probable cause."

"I'm practicing," she said. "The chief said I could," she quickly pointed out.

I told her, "They can see you. When you're logged in, and I try to log in? It records that."

Later that evening, I secretly emailed the GHSP auditor about what was going on because I had to think about my own ass, not hers. Besides, I think the chief was doing a pretty good job of that anyway.

Two weeks later, I walked in the PD to find Allison straddled over the chief. His office door was wide open and nobody seemed to be around. When I opened the door, I saw the two of them lip locked. The door separating the City Hall from the police department had been locked, so I hoped to just sneak in, grab the keys to the speed trailer, and leave undetected. Chief White spotted me creeping past the door, and said, "Somebody's here."

Allison froze dead where she ... sat. She and the chief held their breaths and listened for any movement. I tried to cover my laugh with my hands, but couldn't. I almost laughed myself into peeing all over the place. I knew he had heard me, so I asked, "What are you doing in there, Chief?"

I could hardly contain myself. I was laughing so hard I cried, and my bladder was just moments from bursting.

"I'll be out in a minute," Chief White said.

I thought that was the perfect opportunity for a little payback, so I said, "Hey chief? Your wife's here."

He panicked. "Where's she at?"

"Walking up the sidewalk. Gotta go." I replied, and then quickly grabbed my clipboard and hurried out the door, leaving the chief and Allison to ponder what Betty, Chief White's wife, would do. Even better than that, to ponder what the chief would say when he figured out Betty wasn't there.

Later that evening, I told Dailey what I had seen. Then Dailey told me the chief had already contacted him to ask whether I had said anything to him about what I saw.

CHAPTER 3

YOU ARE THE CLOSEST THING TO PERFECT

A few days or so later, I was logged in to my MySpace account and noticed I had a new friend request from a young lady with the unusual screen name, *You're The Closest Thing to Perfect.*

The next day, I was at Kopp's Quik Stop and was talking to Buddy when this girl showed up with a much older man. Buddy spoke to her and I recognized her face, but I just couldn't place her. I was leaning back against the driver's door of my patrol vehicle. A small crowd had gathered around Buddy and me. The girl plowed her way through and, I'll never forget this, she was wearing an orange *Where's the beef?* T-shirt tied in a knot on her side. She wore blue jean shorts and had on rabbit fur boots with furry dice hanging off the sides.

When she made it through the crowd to my patrol car, she said, "I'm Brittany. I'm in your friends list on MySpace." I almost burst into laughter as I recalled Buddy's impression of her.

Buddy had already told me that they broke up again, and I just said, "Hello."

Brittany's father, the older man, walked out of the store, and said, "Let's go Brittany." Brittany hugged Buddy, and then reached for me. I pulled back, and then Brittany said, "I'm not going to bite you."

After that brief encounter, Brittany began to send me numerous emails through MySpace. There was nothing too unusual, at least, not at first.

A few days later, Brittany requested a ride-along form from the chief. She asked when I would be on duty next because she and Buddy wanted to ride with me.

All the officers had police business cards with the police cell phone number printed on the face. Whoever was on duty carried the cell phone. When the chief left the police department for a period of time, the department's phone was forwarded to dispatch or to the police cell phone.

Brittany called and asked if she could do her ride-along that same evening. I told her to meet me at the police department because the chief had to approve the ride-along. Brittany was already there when I arrived. As I pulled in the parking lot, I recognized Brittany's father, Johnny, standing just outside the front door of the PD. He was smoking a cigarette.

"How ya doing?" I asked as I walked past. Johnny could only nod his head because he was taking a draw from his cigarette.

"This is Brittany Lewis," Chief White said when I walked inside. "She said you told her to meet you here for a ride along?"

I turned to find Brittany sitting in a chair in the waiting area. Brittany smiled and waved, "Remember me," she asked.

I asked whether she had turned in her permission request form. She pointed at the chief, "He has it." Johnny walked in then and asked, "Do you need anything else from me?"

Chief White looked up from reading Brittany's permission slip and asked her, "Are you sixteen?"

Brittany nodded her head yes and looked over to her dad. He said, "She's sixteen."

The chief handed me her permission slip and told Brittany to have fun. Moments later, the chief left. I gave Brittany a quick tour of the PD and City Hall. I showed her where everyone's office was, and then I showed her the evidence room. The evidence room was just a medium-sized walk-in closet with standup lockers on the right and file cabinets on the left. I opened the two lockers containing all the seized drugs and guns.

I handed her a sealed evidence bag and said, "That's an eight-ball of cocaine." Brittany's eyes opened wide as half-dollar coins. "Wow," she said. I stowed the coke away, locked the file cabinets, and secured the door. Then we headed out to make some traffic stops.

CHIEF WHITE'S PRISONER

We hadn't even made out of the parking lot before Chief White requested my assistance on West Boiling Springs Road. When I got there, I recognized Chief

White's prisoner, a young man I had seen at a small barbecue cookout held at Robert's Auto in town. Even though Robert, the owner of the auto shop, had a criminal record, I hadn't let that stop me from introducing myself. I told him the same thing I told others in his situation, "Everyone makes mistakes," I'd say, then I'd add, "I just never got caught."

I had met Robert, his daughter Lisa, and her boyfriend Danny, shortly after I was hired on at the BSL PD. Lisa handled the counter at the auto shop and Danny was one of the mechanics. I often hung out at the garage, both on and off duty. I'd narrate the prior night's entertainment about the dumbest criminals.

On this particular evening, Chief White's prisoner, Bob, was related to Robert. Bob was young and he also had a minor criminal past. He was sitting on an old, discarded concrete block that was lying on its side in the ditch alongside the road. He was covered with dirt, he was bleeding, and he was handcuffed. His dirt bike was pitched on its side in the ditch. As I exited my vehicle, I told Brittany, "Stay in the car until I figure out what's going on."

The chief met me at my side of my car. "Charge him with everything you can think of, from no operator's license to no inspection sticker," he said.

I explained to the chief that I hadn't witnessed any of those crimes. I said, "This is your traffic stop. I can't write him tickets."

"If anybody says anything, I'll tell them I told you to write the tickets," the chief replied.

Seeing how mad the chief was, I calculated that bucking him any farther wouldn't be a good idea right then, so I said, "Tell me what happened then."

"I watched that son-of-a-bitch cross over the highway, and when I got behind him, he tried to run."

West Boiling Springs Road was unmarked pavement for about a quarter-mile and then it turned into a dirt road, full of pot holes for the next five or six miles. Some of those holes were so deep that when it rained enough, water would cover the hood on most vehicles that tried to pass. That portion of West Boiling Springs Road was abandoned for the most part, which made for perfect dirt bike trails.

"How did he get so messed up?" I asked.

"I rammed his ass!" Chief White replied.

The City Manager, Dave Lewis, was sitting in the passenger seat of the chief's patrol vehicle. Dave, a Harry Potter look-alike, stared straight-ahead clutching his leather business pouch against his chest. At the same time I noticed Dave in the chief's car, Brittany leaned across the front seat. Looking out the driver's side window she asked, "Can I get out now?"

I nodded my head yes then bent down to inspect Dave's expression more closely. "What'd the boss say?" I asked the chief.

"Nothing. I told him to turn his damn head," he answered.

I went over to Bob and removed the chief's handcuffs, noticing the impressions they had left on Bob's wrist, just from the chief's temper.

I handed Bob my own shiny pair of new handcuffs and said, "Put these on." Dave pushed his glasses up on his face but his eyes remained fixated on a small spot on the windshield. "Here's your cuffs back," I said as I tossed them to Chief White.

"Charge that son-of-a-bitch with everything you can think of, alright? I mean everything," the chief said.

"Okay, Chief." I replied.

Chief White, with Dave beside him, quickly pulled away after making sure I put Bob in the back of my patrol car.

I took my time with Bob and waited until Chief White was far enough out of sight. When I was sure the chief was gone, I told Bob, "Slide back out so I can take those off." I smiled and dangled a set of cuff keys between my forefingers. While I freed Bob from the cuffs, I asked him, "Why in the world did you run from the chief?"

"I didn't." Bob said. "I didn't know he was behind me until he rammed me."

Chief White and Bob had been about half a mile back in the woods, not too far from some power lines. They had already passed several trails that Bob could've taken to lose the chief. His dirt bike was loud. The other officers and I had all warned the chief that his siren did not work properly and couldn't be heard beyond about 200 feet.

Despite my personal beliefs, I wrote the citations. I told Bob, "Here's what I'm going to do. I have to write a few tickets. I don't have a choice in that. I'll push the court dates way out so you can get an attorney. The rest is up to your attorney. Have him call me."

"That'll work." Bob replied.

"How's April?" I asked him. He said that she was fine, and then we wrapped up our business.

I later monitored Bob's progress through the court's website. When his court dates came due, I had counter-attacks of my own. I simply failed to show up for court, anticipating the prosecutor would dismiss the citation without calling me.

If she did, I was ready to say, "Just dismiss it. Something came up and I'm out of town on urgent business."

She did call as it turned out. As if my first response wasn't good enough, she asked, "You don't want to reschedule it?"

"No," I told her, and added, "Just dismiss it. I can use him sometime down the road anyway."

●

Now, I know some might suggest that my conduct was an abuse of power, but in one form or another, you'll soon discover that I often found ways to balance the scales of justice and equality. I'm sure the chief got real pissed off when he found out I dismissed all Bob's charges, but I looked at it like this: My signature was on his citations as the officer who witnessed the crimes. I had witnessed nothing. Hell, I guess you could say that if I wasn't pissing off the chief … I was pissing on him.

●

So I let Bob go, and then Brittany and I patrolled Hwy. 87 for a while. She spilled the beans about her life, how she was somehow related to Judge Lewis, her parents separating, and her mother's new career choice; prostitution. Brittany told me her mother had gotten a staph infection and gonorrhea from her dad and that's why they were divorcing. She went on to tell me her father had molested her in the past, but now that he had a girlfriend, all that had stopped. Brittany described how she had tried to cut her wrists. She said her parents didn't believe she was really trying to kill herself because the cuts were not deep enough. I didn't know whether to believe her or not. Some kids say things to get attention. Regardless, I was required to make a report.

I just logged it in like any other call for service:

```
POLICE PAK

Report Type: Call for Service - Law Enforcement
Officer Entry

Officer: 1177 BSL UNIT

Officer L. Stidham had a ride-along participate
named Brittany Lewis, a 16-year-old female, for
approx. three hours. Brittany informed LEO that
her father had molested her in the past, but
had stopped after father-acquired girlfriend.
Victim said she could not remember dates.
Victim stated father had groped her breast when
she was getting out of the shower. Victim
became suspicious of LEO asking questions.
Unable to determine facts at this time. Victim
also stated that she had tried to hurt herself
in the past. Admitted self-inflicting cuts to
wrist.

Faxed to DA's office for follow up.
```

I gave Brittany one of my police business cards and told her to call me if she ever felt like hurting herself again. The next evening, she called.

A DECEPTIVE KISS

"Hey, do you know who this is?" an almost familiar voice asked.

"No, not right off," I replied.

"Brittany, from yesterday."

"Oh, okay," I said. "What's up?"

"You said that I could call you if I needed to talk, right?"

"Yeah."

"Can you meet me at the park?"

"Sure," I replied. "What's going on?"

"Can you meet me now?" Brittany whispered into the phone.

"Yeah, but what's going on?"

"I'll tell you at the park." Brittany said, and with a click she was gone.

As I turned into the parking area at the park, I saw Brittany swinging, but another girl accompanied her. I pulled up close to the swing set and rolled down the driver's window. Brittany jumped out of the swing in mid-flight and ran up to the window.

"What's up?" I asked.

"I can't talk right now." Brittany replied.

"Why not?"

Brittany nodded her head toward her girlfriend, an obese female around 17-years-old, who was just swinging back and forth.

"What does she have to do with what you have to tell me?" I asked.

I believe Brittany could hear the skepticism in my voice because in a pleading voice she said, "I didn't think she would come with me. Can I just call you later?"

I paused a few seconds examining her expression, then asked, "Is everything all right with you?"

Brittany turned and ran back to the swings, as I called out, "Hey, just so you know, if I don't answer, that means I'm busy. Just call back later."

"Okay." Brittany replied. She waved and skipped along like a little schoolgirl who just won a spelling bee. She turned back and then asked, "Oh, wait, can I give you a hug?"

I've had countless hugs in my life so her request didn't seem unusual. "What did I do to deserve this?" I asked, as she ran back up to my window.

"You're the only one who's nice to me," she said.

I leaned out through the window, and after Brittany hugged me, she snuck in a quick kiss on my cheek.

"All righty then," I said, "Didn't see that coming."

Brittany laughed and skipped away.

A FALSIFIED TICKET

About three days later, I responded to a call about a vehicle accident involving a motorcycle and a Toyota Celica. The accident had occurred right in front of the police department. The motorcycle had been traveling west on Hwy 87 and was following a truck. The Celica was stopped at an intersection and was going to turn left off East Boiling Springs Road onto Hwy 87 and headed east. The truck slowed to make a right-hand turn onto East Boiling Springs Road. The motorcycle merged left of the centerline to overcome and pass the truck. At the same time, the Celica made a left-hand turn. The motorcycle crashed into the left side of the car.

I was inside the police department filing a B&E report when the call came in from dispatch. It was police policy to run the blue lights and face on-coming traffic when we were on an accident scene, so I pulled off the east side of the road facing west on George II Hwy. The motorcycle was still wedged between the driver's front tire and fender.

"That bitch pulled right out in front of me!" Eric, the driver of the motorcycle said, pointing to the driver of the Toyota Celica.

I was immediately offended, so I fired back, "You ain't going to do that. Stand right there and don't move!"

Then I asked, "Do either of you need a medic?"

Both drivers shook their heads no. They were still bickering some, so I had to separate the two. I walked around the scene and took a few notes. I stepped off the tire marks left by the motorcycle. I was satisfied that I had figured out who was at fault, but I still wanted to hear at least one driver's version of what had happened, so I approached Brenda, the driver of the Celica first.

"Tell me what happened."

"I saw the truck turning right onto East Boiling Springs Road, so I turned left. The motorcycle was right there and hit me. He was right in the middle of the road."

I motioned for Eric to join us and said, "Here's the deal. I am going to issue you both a citation because both of you are at fault."

"What the hell did I do?" Eric challenged.

I explained that he crossed left of the centerline attempting to pass and overcome the vehicle in front of him in a no passing zone. Brenda had failed to yield to oncoming traffic. "Just because a driver had the blinker on, doesn't give either of you the right-of-way to pull out," I said.

The following Monday, the chief called me to come in on my day off. "Get your ass in here and rewrite these accident reports!"

"Hold up, Chief! Who you talk'n to like that? I'm off duty and your payroll." I responded. "And what's wrong with my report?"

"Just get in here when you can," he replied.

When I arrived, Officer Felts was busy washing his patrol vehicle. He stopped long enough to say, "He sure is pissed off at chu boy."

"Fuck him, I don't care." I said. "What's wrong with my tickets?"

"Noth'n I seen, but what I overheard him saying, I think that motorcycle guy is a friend da his." Felts replied. He was an old school country boy with the belly to match. He spat a mouth full of tobacco juice on his windshield and then said, "It cleans tha bugs off tha winders."

"That was sick." I replied. The mere sight of spit made me queasy. "Thanks, now I'm going to gag."

I walked fearlessly across the parking lot and up the sidewalk, gagging the whole way, where the chief waited at the door.

"What's wrong with my reports?" I asked.

"Rewrite both reports; the motorcycle is not at fault. He swerved to miss the other car. Didn't they teach you anything in rookie school?" the chief said, then repeated, "Rewrite it."

"He is at fault. The motorcycle sped up to pass the truck on the left. They made contact in the left turn lane," I said. "What more do you need?"

"I said rewrite it, and yes, that's an order."

I guess by now he knew I would ask, so I said, "Okay. I'll rewrite 'em, your version then mine."

"No, you're going to rewrite the report excluding the motorcycle of fault, and then you're going to take him a copy of it," Chief White said.

"Oh. Now I get it," I said. "You know him don't you?"

"This is not open for discussion," he said.

Chief White took a long gulp from his coffee mug. A standoff between him and me commenced, then the front door swung open, and in walked Brittany.

What the chief proposed was illegal. How can this asshole make me rewrite a report that I know is false? I debated to myself.

Not wanting Brittany to hear our confrontation, I said, "No problem, Chief, I'll fix it." The chief briefly spoke with Brittany while I rewrote the tickets as "*ordered*." I noticed that the chief swiftly wrote down directions to Eric's house before handing it to me, and then he said, "Take her with you." He looked back at Brittany and said, "That's what happens when someone doesn't do their job."

Brittany looked at me and asked, "What'd you do?"

I gave no response. As I walked past her, I said, "Let's go."

Eric lived just down the road from the PD, and when I handed him a new accident report, he said, "I've known the chief all my life; he said he'd take care of this."

"Is that right?" I asked. "This is the chief's version of what happened, not mine," I said, already turning and walking away from him.

Brittany had gotten out of the car so I had to wait for her to catch up. When she closed her door I said, "I'm ill and I'm not on duty. I don't know why the chief told me to take you with me, but stay in the car from here on out."

"Are you mad at me?" she asked.

"No, at someone else."

When I returned to the police department, I left Brittany in the car, and went inside where I confronted the chief. "You didn't bother telling me Eric's known you all his life. Maybe next time you should get your wires straight, and I will be dismissing the other driver's ticket."

"You do and you'll be pushing a pencil." Chief White responded.

Brenda, the driver of the Celica, was also local to BSL. To even the score, I also pushed her new court date way out. Without saying much else, I delivered Brenda the new ticket. As she opened the door, I said, "I dismissed your first ticket. Here's a new one ... for now. I pushed your court date out to March of next year. If your insurance company needs the accident report, just have 'em contact me, and only me."

As I walked back to my patrol car, I saw Brittany on a cell phone. I didn't pay much attention to it at first, until we were headed back to the police department. I glanced down to locate the police cell phone.

"Here," Brittany said, handing me the phone she'd been using.

"You were on my phone?" I asked.

"I thought it was okay," she said.

"What made you think that?"

I was already irritated and finding her on my phone made matters worse.

"I didn't know but…whatever," she said. "Just take me home."

"No," I said. "I picked you up at the PD and that's where I'm dropping you off."

Later on, Brenda's attorney called me about the new ticket. *Now it's my turn.* I thought. "What ticket?" I asked.

As luck would have it, Brenda's attorney had received her original accident report … from an anonymous donor.

CHAPTER 4

MULTIPLE UNKNOWN INJURIES

I returned to duty on the following Wednesday. By late evening, Brittany had called repeatedly, asking to go on a ride-along. "I have something important to talk to you about," she said.

"Is it an emergency?" I asked.

She said it wasn't, so I told her maybe some other time would be better for another ride-along, but I said that she could call later.

I drove to the far north end of BSL and parked at Olde Brunswick General Store and set up to run radar. I knew if I did that at Kopp's Quik Stop, Brittany would see me and walk over, asking again to ride with me. About an hour later, I received a call from dispatch.

"Have report of a ten-fifty on the corner of Fifty Lakes and George II Hwy. Caller reported multiple unknown injuries. Possible vehicle fire. Have medical and fire en route."

"Ten-four. Show me en route," I responded.

Olde Brunswick General Store sat on the corner of Hwy 133 and the north end of Fifty Lakes Drive. The south end of Fifty Lakes was only about a ten-minute drive under normal conditions. I made it in less than five. I was the first responding officer.

The accident scene looked bad. A white Jeep Cherokee was lying on its side facing west. A small amount of smoke was coming from under its hood. Bits and pieces of a motorcycle were lying all over the road and in a trail that led off toward the edge of the woods. Ron, the driver of the Jeep, walked up beside me, blood running down the left side of his head.

"My wife's disabled," he said, "She's trapped in the Jeep."

At that moment, I was opening the back of my patrol vehicle. I was nervous and my heart pounded. I strapped on the reflective vest and then unlocked my fire extinguisher.

"Did you hear me?" Ron asked in an elevate voice.

"Yes sir, I heard you. I'm coming."

As I started to cross the road, I paused and tried to recall my training. I scanned the area and looked for other vehicles that could have been involved. My heart still pounded out of control. This was one of the types of calls I regretted; my hands even trembled. I had always feared that someone might die from my rookie mistakes.

Officer Dailey often monitored the police radio and would call to offer his assistance. A sense of relief came over me as my police cell rang.

"Hey, it's me."

"Brittany?" I asked disappointed.

"Yeah, it's me," she replied. "What's wrong with you?"

"I'll have to call you back," I told her, hanging up quickly. I noticed a second vehicle that had clearly been in the accident. A blue, early 70's model Chevy Capri had pulled out and had t-boned the Jeep Cherokee. A motorcycle had been traveling behind the Jeep, and a guy named Charlie, the driver of the motorcycle, had locked up his back brakes, sliding into the right, rear corner of the Jeep and causing the motorcycle and him to flip end over end. The motorcycle finally came to rest about 30 yards in the woods. Charlie was nowhere to be found.

"My brother was behind me on a motorcycle." Ron said. "I think he hit me pretty hard."

Ron looked around and found pieces of Charlie's motorcycle strewn across the road. "This is all part of his motorcycle," he said. His voice quivered with fear.

"Let me go check on the driver of the blue car," I said.

As I started running to the Capri, dispatch called. "C-COM, eleven seventy-seven? Is everything ten-four?"

"Negative, I need medics, ten-eighteen traffic. I have one driver missing and one occupant trapped so far. No vehicle fire at this time but keep fire coming."

Almost forgetting where I was headed, I paused a second before starting toward the Capri again. There was no movement inside the car. As I approached the passenger's door, I saw a baby that was crying, strapped in a car seat in the back seat.

The mother, a blonde-haired woman, was face down against the steering wheel. I grabbed the handle of the passenger side door and tried to open it, but it had been jammed by the collision. I ran around to the driver's side, only to find that door handle was gone, missing.

I slipped and then slammed down, hard, on the pavement as I dashed back around the front of the car. As I got back on my feet, I cut the corner and then grabbed the passenger's door handle. I yanked hard, again and again, bracing myself with my foot.

"Are you okay?" I yelled, as I banged my fist against the window. "Hey! Can you hear me?"

"Eleven seventy-seven, C-COM?" I frantically called.

"C-COM, go ahead."

"I have two additional trapped occupants, one is an infant. I need rescue. Where's my medic?" I began fearing for the lives of three people now.

Dispatch answered, but in my adrenaline overload, I never heard a word. With my baton cocked over my head, my police cell phone rang. *Maybe that's Dailey.* I hoped. Although we had our issues, he had a lot more experience than me.

I answered the phone, only to hear, "I thought you were going to call me back."

"Brittany?" I asked.

"Yeah."

"I will later. I'm busy. Can't talk, 'bye." I couldn't have made it simpler than that and now for the second time, I had hung up on her.

I needed help, and I needed it fast. I scrolled through the contact list, searching for Officer Dailey. A blunt tone told me that his cell phone was turned off.

I raised back my baton and struck the window; the glass shattered into a web of cracks. A second swing broke through the window. Bracing the baton with both hands, I raked loose what few barbed edges remained, or so I thought.

"Lady!" I shouted. "Hey Lady! Can you hear me?" I laid the baton on the top of the car, and crawled through the window. I braced myself with one hand with my feet dangling outside. I reached over with the other hand and checked for a pulse. I was shaking so bad that I couldn't determine what I was feeling.

"Was that me or you?" I asked, and then held my breath and remained as still as I could.

The impact had catapulted her head against the steering wheel, knocking her unconscious. *Thank God.* I thought as I welcomed the signs of life between my forefingers. I hadn't realized that the shards of glass had cut my hand until I reached over the back seat and grabbed the baby's hand. The baby was crying but appeared to be unharmed.

I had crawled over the back seat by then and realized that I could've just opened the back door. As I got out, I looked around the car searching for gas leaks, and then I noticed that I had ripped my pants leg in the window.

I crossed back over the road to search for the driver of the motorcycle. Medics and a convoy of the fire department's vehicles rolled up. Looking into the fire truck as it approached, I saw Buddy, appearing to be on his cell phone.

I opened his door and said, "I have three trapped. One adult in the Jeep. One adult, one infant in the Capri. The blood on the baby's mine. The driver of the motorcycle is missing."

"Brittany is mad as hell at you," Buddy said, stepping down from the mammoth-sized fire truck.

"What the hell are you talking about?" I asked.

"She said you keep hanging up on her."

"I'm on a damn accident call."

"I know, but that's the way she is."

"What is she thinking ... that I am her boyfriend or something?" I asked. "That little girl makes me glad I can't have kids anymore."

"What?" Buddy asked laughing, "You been clipped?"

"Hell yeah! Clipped, snipped, and burned, baby. Nothing but blanks," I replied. "You better not tell nobody either," I said, as I held up my hand to show Buddy the blood.

Including Buddy, about 10 BSL firemen arrived on scene. Buddy and I ran to the Jeep to assist the disabled woman. The remaining firemen began to assist the mother and infant in the Capri. The Jaws of Life cut through the metal doors and peeled back the roof like a sardine can.

"Is Brittany a trouble maker?" I asked.

"Why do you think I broke up with her? You can never believe anything she says," Buddy said.

"She called me several days ago, acting like she had some kind of urgent matter and must talk to..." I paused when I saw Buddy's gesture. "What?"

Buddy was shaking his head and finished the thought, "And when you got there, she said she couldn't talk because someone was with her or her dad was coming."

"That's exactly what happened." I said.

Buddy examined my hand for glass and then wrapped it in a bandage. He and I helped the disabled woman from the Jeep and carried her a safe distance away. Ron ran up and met us just as we started searching in the woods for Charlie.

"Sir, I need for you to stay back." I said holding up my hands. "Go see the medics. I'll find you when I find your brother."

All of a sudden, Ron froze. His eyes fixed on an object lying about 10 yards behind Buddy. I got that sudden, unmistakable fear that something horrible was behind me. The hairs on the back of my neck stood up; chills ran down my arms and legs. "He's right over there." Ron said, and he collapsed to his knees.

"Just point where he's at." I said.

Ron lifted his hand and pointed behind us.

"I'll be right back, okay? Stay here." I said.

My cell phone rang again. The caller ID displayed: "Private Incoming Call." I couldn't believe it. "You've got to be freakin' kidding me." I said.

"That's probably, Brittany." Buddy said.

"It better not be."

"I'll put a hundred dollars on it," Buddy offered.

"Police department!" I said sternly.

"Don't hang up on me," a female's voice said.

"Is this Brittany?" I asked.

"Yes," she replied, "Why are you mad at me?"

"I ain't mad, yet. I'm working. I have injuries! I'll call you!" But then it hit me about the caller ID. "Wait, did you just block your number?" I then asked with a ton of sarcasm.

"No," she replied softly.

"Did you call me from the same number you called before?" I was nearly shouting into the phone.

"Whatever. Just call me back, I really need to talk to you." Brittany said, and with a click she was gone again.

"Who does she think she is?" I asked.

Buddy replied laughing, "Better you than me."

The medics and firemen rescued all the remaining wounded occupants. A second and third ambulance arrived on scene as back up. The baby and her mother were transported together to Dosher Hospital. Ron rode with his wife, and they were transported to Brunswick Hospital.

Charlie's body was discovered tangled up in a briar patch about 10 yards behind us. His legs were twisted and turned in unnatural ways. His left arm was broken backwards at the elbow, with the skin torn and ripped from his arm and exposing the bloody bone. I found Charlie's head about 10 minutes later, still strapped in his helmet. His head had rolled nearly 25 yards into a ditch. When Charlie hit the Jeep, his upper torso slammed against the back of the Jeep. His body spun wildly into the air. A directional highway sign then decapitated him.

For some stupid reason, right before I picked up his head, I lifted his visor. "Holy shit!" I said, and then quickly slammed the visor back. He was staring right at me. Chills ran up my arms to my neck again. I placed Charlie's head in a plastic grocery bag and then carried it back to his body. The Coroner arrived on scene and zipped Charlie's head up in the bag with his body. That was a horrible night, but for a police officer, especially a new one, it's hard to just pick back up and go back on your regular beat.

CHAPTER 5

THE SEDUCTION BEGINS

After I wrapped up the accident scene, I returned Brittany's phone call. Her voicemail picked up.

"This is Luke, You need to call back right now." Two minutes later the police cell phone rang.

"Hey," Brittany replied.

A few moments of silence passed and then Brittany asked, "Whatcha doing?"

I laid the phone down by my side, feeling like I just wanted to explode. I was so emotionally exhausted, and somehow, could still see Charlie's dead eyes.

I took a couple of long deep breaths before lifting the phone back up, "Do you have something to talk to me about?" I asked, trying to hide my impatience.

"It was about my dad and Buddy, but whatever. I was able to fix it myself." Brittany said, and then she asked, "Can I go on a ride-along tonight? Oh, and um, you know, so I'm a bitch and I make you glad you can't have kids, huh?"

"Thanks Buddy." I said. "And I never called you a bitch." I rubbed my forehead, disgusted, and then asked, "I guess Buddy told you that?"

"That wasn't very nice, you know. But whatever." Brittany said.

"I didn't call you a bitch, Brittany."

"You just said you did."

"No, I said I guess Buddy … just never mind. Does he tell you everything we talk about?"

"Pretty much," she replied. "Did you really have surgery?"

"Oh that's just fucking great!" I replied.

"Did it hurt?"

"No." I replied. "Why?" I felt her questions were a bit intrusive, and I guess Brittany heard that in my voice because she paused before continuing.

"Just wondering." Then she changed the subject, "Oh, did you see my new pictures on MySpace?"

"No. What are they?"

"Me and Buddy, and I took pictures of you riding down the road in your police car."

"You put me on the Internet?" I asked.

"Yeah. Are you mad?"

"That's not cool, Brittany."

"I'll take them down," she said. "Just go look at them first."

"I will later. And listen to me very carefully, I will ... call ... you ... later, okay? I'll call you! And no ride-along tonight."

CHAPTER 6

SUICIDE KID

It had been several days since I had last heard from Brittany, and by now she, as well as everyone else, had figured out my work schedule. It was the same routine: two days on, two day off, three days on, two days off. That gave each officer a three-day weekend every other week.

It was a warm summer day in 2005. Officer Dailey was the primary officer on duty. I was the secondary. We received a call for a ten ninety-six. That's a call most officers fear, even with backup—Shots fired. While we were en route, we got another call from dispatch.

"C-COM, eleven seventy-five? Seventy-seven? Your ten ninety-six is a male subject. Appears to be self-inflicting."

I was second to arrive on scene. Still new to the game, my heart pounded and felt like it was about to burst from my chest. I wondered if I was ready to see another dead body. And a suicide at that. All I could think about was whether he had suffered.

As I walked up the driveway, I heard crying and screaming coming from the house. Officer Dailey pointed to a car parked inside a small garage. The driver's door was open and I could see the left leg of a young male dangling.

"Self-inflicted—suicide," Dailey said.

I froze. Still a good 10 feet away from the car, I had to force my legs to carry me forward, all the time I was thinking, *I don't want to see this*. I approached the driver's side of the car, leaned in, and there he was. I could see the head shot wound - center of the forehead. His eyes were locked looking upward as if he were looking for God's forgiveness. His brain had swelled from the trauma. It slowly seeped from the wound. Just as quick as I leaned in, I turned away. I became nauseous and weak. The cries I heard earlier got closer.

"Is he dead?" Came a female's voice from behind me.

I couldn't speak, not yet anyway. It took a second before I could even look at her. I was still in shock. I'd never seen a suicide before. The lump in my throat grew until it felt like I was choking on a baseball. She must have read my facial expression or body language, but either way, she got her answer. She held her stomach, turned, and walked back to the small crowd of mourners now gathered just outside the garage.

That's the only moment when I wished the people of BSL didn't feel so comfortable around me. I knew they looked to me as the "good cop," but I still didn't want them to see me so disturbed.

"He's dead! He's not moving!" the woman cried in horror. "Andy!"

I walked around to the passenger's side, trying to keep my composure. I took a second look. The impact of the bullet had cracked the entire right side of his skull and it was just lying in place like a lid to a canning jar. The swelling of the brain broke its seal, and then it slowly lifted up.

I was examining the rear of the car when my police cell phone rang.

"Hey baby."

"Brittany?" I asked.

"Whatcha doing?"

"Working a shooting scene right now," I said. "And did you just call me 'baby?'

"Yeah," she said laughing. "Call me back. Bye." And with another click she was gone again.

After I examined the rear of the car more thoroughly, I discovered that the exit wound had blown brain matter all over the back seat. His head laid against the headrest and turned to his right a little. It looked as if he was just sleeping, but with his eyes open. Brain matter and blood pooled on the rear floorboard. The forty-five-caliber rifle still laid in his lap with his right thumb gripping the trigger.

Dailey walked up and removed the rifle from his lap. Hell, I didn't know what to do. I had momentarily forgotten all my training and was useless at that point. Everything seemed to move in slow motion. This boy must've been in his early twenties.

"Maybe he didn't mean to pull the trigger." I said.

"He meant to pull the trigger. Are you okay?" Officer Dailey asked. "Man up. You gotta get used to this kind of thing."

"Don't tell me to man up!" I said, offended. "I've just never seen a suicide before."

Dailey said, "Besides, his father was a suicide too; like father like son."

I leaned up, "You are one sick son-of-a-bitch. You know that?"

Dailey tried to sugar-coat his ill-mannered gesture, "I was joking, Luke."

I found no humor in that and rolled my eyes. Officer Dailey was cruel in everything he said and did. It was no wonder the people of BSL hated him so much.

By the time the Coroner came and bagged the body, Brittany had called back a dozen or more times, but after about her third attempt, I sent her calls to voicemail. As I watched, the Coroner pulled the young man's body from the car. His hands, arms, and legs were locked in place; frozen in a position that suggested he was still sitting in his car. The Coroner had to forcibly move his arms and legs to maneuver his body around. I heard things pop and snap in his body, and that really shook me up.

My heart broke. My brain was on overload. *Maybe I'm not cut out for this?* I wondered. So many other questions ran through my head. My imagination played a picture of him pulling the trigger.

The scene looked like a suicide, but we still had to assume all available possibilities.

"I want to get a swiping of everyone's hand for gunshot residue." Officer Dailey said.

As cruel as that sounded, we had a job to do. We had to secure the scene. No one could leave until we got a statement and a hand swipe from everyone. Although this upset the family and friends, I believe they all accepted it as protocol.

Dailey would interview each person alone, then I'd interview them. I interviewed Shannon Iceland, the younger brother. Shannon was 13-years-old. He was a lanky boy. I took notes as he talked.

"We were all inside the house and Andy had been on the phone arguing with his girlfriend. After he hung up, he walked outside."

"Did you hear the conversation?" I asked.

"Not really," he said, "His girlfriend's dad didn't like him so that was probably what it was about."

"Where did he keep the rifle?" I asked.

"He kept it under his bed. I don't know how he got it out without me seeing him. A few minutes after he went outside, I heard two popping sounds. 'Pop!' And then about a minute later, 'Pop!' Like that. I thought Andy was working on his car or something. About 10 minutes later, we all left to go to Kopp's, and after we got back, I could see his leg hanging from the door. I didn't know that he'd shot himself." Shannon said.

His bottom lip quivered. "I called out his name, but he didn't answer. I kept saying 'Andy! Andy!' Usually if he was mad or something he would yell back, 'What the hell you want?' But he didn't. I walked up to his car and that's when," he covered his face.

"I know it hurts Shannon." I said. I could only imagine how he felt. I placed my hand on his shoulder. "We'll get through this." I added.

"That's when I saw the gun and the hole, in his, in his head." Shannon said.

Shannon's heartache overwhelmed him as he sobbed wildly for his brother. His mother was all he had left. Shannon laid his head on my shoulder. My pen and notepad dropped carelessly to the ground when I wrapped both arms around him. I felt the trembling of Shannon's ribs as he mourned.

As I held on to Shannon, my phone rang several times. I didn't take the time to find out whom it was, but I assumed that it was Brittany.

Dailey and I finished up our report and then we left. Dailey closed the case as a suicide.

THE TENDER VOICE OF OLD MRS. BAILEY

A couple weeks later, I received a call from dispatch about a person requesting officer's assistance. Usually when those types of calls came in, it was someone looking to ask the officer questions about law or they had another simple complaint. When I arrived at the home, I spotted an elderly lady sitting on the front porch. I notified dispatch that I was on scene and proceeded to approach. As I got closer, I noticed her crying. *Domestic violence* was the first thing that came to mind.

"Can I help you?" I stated as kindly as I knew how. At first she didn't answer, "Are you okay?" I asked.

There was a small knee-high wall between us. I was standing on the outside of her porch, and she was sitting on a bench.

"I want to die." She finally said.

"Tell me why," I said, hoping to keep her talking, but she shook her head, avoiding eye contact with me.

By then I could tell she was intoxicated, making the situation even more dangerous for her and myself. I walked just past the knee wall and that's when a small handgun came into view. It was lying on the deck at her feet. I was now in great danger; how I reacted over the next few seconds would determine both our futures.

"There is nothing more I want than to help you figure out what it is that can be so bad that you want to end your life," I said gently. Meanwhile, my police cell phone rang. I looked down, saw it was Brittany. I switched it to voicemail, then to vibrate.

Whenever Mrs. Bailey looked away, I snapped my fingers and said, "Right here, I'm right here. I'll listen. Try me." I walked slowly until I was right on top of the gun. I believe she was too intoxicated to remember she even had it, but I wasn't taking any chances.

As I turned to my right to look off into the woods, the phone vibrated again, but this time, I was in a make-it-or-break-it type situation, so I casually flipped it open and turned it off.

I then pointed off into the woods and asked, "Who is that?" and then I looked back at her. When she looked away, I leaped for the gun.

A thick-figured, lonely-looking woman with long, shimmering, silver hair, 60-year-old Mrs. Bailey, moved quickly for being intoxicated. She wore last night's gown with white slippers. I got both hands on the gun just nanoseconds before she did, and then jerked it loose. "Click." I heard the striking pin slam down. It scared me so bad that I almost let the gun go.

"I'm so sorry," she cried. "I forgot that was there."

"Is this thing loaded?" I asked, as my heart pounded and I gasped for air.

"I think so," she replied.

I dropped the magazine out of the gun and was relieved to find that it was empty. I racked the chamber and one round popped out and bounced on the deck. It was a 9mm. The gun should have fired, and I wasn't wearing my vest that day. It would have hit me somewhere near my chest.

Some have said that God stopped that bullet from firing. That may be, but what I do know is it probably could've killed me. The bullet had a small indentation where the striking pin hit.

I took the Glock apart, called in the serial number, and waited for a gun permit confirmation. She seemed to sober up pretty quickly after that.

She began complaining how I could've been killed trying to save her. She then asked whether I was going to charge her for the gun. "Not as long as it comes back clean," I said, and then I told her I was going to keep it locked at my police department for 30 days for her safety.

She and I talked over three hours after that. Dispatch called a few times with minor stuff, so I told them to contact the chief. "I'll be ten-six for a while, then possibly ten seventy-two with one female to Dosher Hospital," I said.

I promised Mrs. Bailey, if she would let me take her to the hospital, I would come back and visit and see how she was doing. She agreed, and I let her go inside and pack a few clothes, as I stood posted up in her doorway for my safety.

After we got to Dosher Hospital, I stayed with her until the doctors got her assigned to a bed. "Don't forget the promise you made me," she said. Mrs. Bailey's voice was as pleasing to hear as a small child's in prayer. Holding one hand over my heart and her hand in the other, I bent down and kissed her on the forehead. Satisfied that at least I believed and cared, tears pooled in her eyes. She smiled, and I said, "I promise. I won't forget my promise. I'll see you soon."

As I left the hospital, the chief called me on the radio. "Will you give me a ten twenty-one?"

"Ten four, Chief." I replied. I had forgotten to turn my cell phone back on and knew the chief would not be happy.

"I've been trying to call you," the chief barked when he answered.

"My bad," I said. "Someone kept calling me too much."

"Shit, Luke! A few dozen people have called here for you because you won't answer your damn phone," he said. "Answer the damn phone," he shouted.

"It was turned off, Chief. I had a sui ..."

The chief interrupted saying "I don't care what you had. Do not turn that phone off again!"

"Okay, Chief," I said. I paused for a second but he didn't say anything else, so I hung up.

As I drove back to BSL from Southport, I couldn't get Mrs. Bailey off my mind, and as you may already suspect, my phone started ringing off the hook. It was Brittany, of course. I didn't feel much like conversation with anyone, so I sent her to voicemail again.

As I turned back on Hwy 87, I thought about what Mrs. Bailey had shared with me. She told me she felt she had been completely abandoned by her family. She told me that no one lived close enough to come visit, or it was too much trouble to drive. She said her kids argued over her life insurance policy. I was determined to make good on my promise, so I entered a reminder in the police cell phone and called the hospital the next day.

"This is Officer Stidham with the Boiling Spring Lakes Police Department, I signed in Mrs. Bailey yesterday. Can you tell if she is doing okay?"

"She's fine. We've transferred her to Brynn Marr Hospital," a female voice said.

I was lucky to get any information since I wasn't family. I took the incident report and wrote down her home telephone number.

Then Brittany called.

"I've been trying call you for two days," she said.

"I know, and you called the chief too." I replied.

"Well, I was worried about you." Brittany explained.

"When I don't answer, that means I'm in a situation where I can't take the call," I said. "Leave a message, and I'll call you back."

"No you won't," she said.

"That's because you don't give me the chance." I said. "And the chief said no ride-along today." I thought I would cut her off before she even had the chance to ask about that.

"I can't go anyway. We're going out to eat tonight," she replied.

Thank God. I thought, and after several seconds of hearing silence, I asked, "Do you have something to tell me?"

"I just wanted to see how you was doing."

I explained that I was fine, and that I had to run several errands. I told her that I was going on vacation the following day and would be out of town.

"Uh, when will you be back?" she asked, sounding disappointed.

"In a few weeks," I replied. "I'll call you when I get back."

"Can I email you?"

"I don't know when I'll be able to get back to you."

"That's fine," she replied, and her attitude perked back up.

It would be nearly two weeks later before I called Mrs. Bailey every day on duty until I got an answer.

"I'm on my way to your house and I just wanted to make sure you're home."

"Yes, I'm home," she said. "Who's calling?"

"Oh, just an old friend," I replied. "See you in a minute."

She was standing on her porch when I turned onto her side street off Fifty Lakes Drive. Her driveway led right off in the center of a right-hand curve.

As I got into view, I watched as she covered her mouth. Before I could even get out of patrol car, she was walking down the steps, waiving one hand, and wiping tears with the other.

"I didn't think you would come," she said. Her mascara ran down her face. She carefully jogged up and wrapped both of her arms around my neck.

"I told you I would come," I said. That was somehow the most rewarding gift I had ever gotten. It was the tender sweet voice of old Mrs. Bailey.

CHAPTER 7

PLANTED EVIDENCE

I was manning a routine license checkpoint on Alten Lennon Road with Dailey. We set up at the south side of the dam on Alten Lennon Road, with woods on both sides of us. The only escape was a service road near the railroad tracks about 50 yards from the checkpoint. We checked a few cars coming through, but for the most part the night was calm. Issuing a citation has always been left to officer discretion. For me, if I wrote a ticket, the person deserved it.

It was about one o'clock that morning when Brittany called.

"Where are you?" she asked.

"At the dam, doing a license check. Why?"

"Cause me and Jee are going to sneak out tonight," she said.

"I don't want to know about this."

Brittany laughed and said, "We're just going for a walk, but don't tell my dad, okay?"

"I don't know anything about this," I repeated.

I was almost ready to pack it up when a black Ford Escort turned the corner and made a quick dash for the service road.

"Gotta go!" I said and hung up.

I jumped in my patrol vehicle, a four wheel drive Ford Expedition, and took off after the Escort. Dailey headed towards Fifty Lakes Drive on the other end trying to cut them off. The driver had made it about a hundred yards in before he got stuck in the sand. I pulled up behind him blaring my lights and siren in all their glory. I opened my door and began my felony traffic stop. Moments later, Dailey's Impala finally came into view. His headlights bounced like a slow motion basketball off in the distance. Lights, no lights; lights, no lights, until he pulled up from the other direction.

There was only the male driver and his passenger in the car. The passenger, a female, held her hands up pushing against the ceiling liner. The driver and passenger appeared to be about 18-years-old. I ordered the driver out, made him lift his shirt and walk backwards to my voice. I then patted him down, cuffed him, and put him in the front seat of my patrol vehicle. Dailey pulled around us and to my right. He got out of his patrol vehicle, drew his weapon, and took cover behind his door to cover me as I ordered the passenger out.

Once we got the passenger out, I ordered her out the same as her driver, handcuffed her, and then secured her in the back seat of my vehicle. I walked next to the driver and asked, "What were you thinking?"

"I don't know," he replied. "I panicked."

"Is your license revoked?" I asked.

"No. I just forgot my wallet."

I couldn't help but laugh as I told him, "All you had to do was drive up to the check point, tell me you forgot your license, and I would have sent you back to get it."

"I didn't know that." He sounded like he was about to cry.

"What's your name?" I asked.

"That's Jordan Miller." Dailey responded, as he walked up.

Jordan interrupted, "I filed a complaint against Dailey for harassment. Now he hates me." Dailey laughed it off.

Both Jordan and his female passenger were young. I decided to just issue a warning ticket to the kid, something else I often did when the situation warranted it, but he still had one more test to pass.

"Jordan, do I have your permission to search your vehicle?"

"It's not my car," he responded.

"Do you have something to hide?" Dailey interrupted.

"No, go ahead and search then." Jordan said.

While I searched the car, I could hear Dailey and Jordan being mouthy towards each other in the background. Many of the people from BSL knew Dailey all too well and referred to him as "Double-O-Dick-Dailey." Jordan's passenger was still in the back of my patrol car and said very little.

I was about to release both kids when Dailey decided to search. Moments later, he emerged from the Escort holding a three inch red straw.

"You didn't do a very good job," he said. "Coke straw. Test it." He dangled the straw in the air and said, "I gotcha now Jordan."

"Where did you find it?" I asked, shocked.

"In the CC," Dailey said, a little too clever for his own good.

•

"CC" is police jargon for center console. It had contained about six items, a bottle of ladies perfume, a tampon, a couple of pens, and some small pieces of papers. The vehicle was clean. This whole situation was just a nervous teenager who'd forgotten his license.

•

I was alarmed at Dailey's suggestion because the center console was just too obvious, but then a shocking realization came to me. I knew, in that instant, the rumors and stories I'd been told about Dailey were confirmed. He had planted that straw. I knew it, and I knew with everything in my heart. I didn't realize just how long I had stared at Dailey thinking, *You planted that, you piece of shit,* until he asked me a second time to test it. I tested it, and of course, it was positive for cocaine.

Dispatch called then, and told me someone had been calling in on a white Durango that was driving wildly on West Boiling Spring Lakes Road.

"Ten-four. I'm busy on a traffic stop, but I'll be en route momentarily," I replied.

Dailey and I argued about who was going to charge them, but I maintained, "I'm not the one who found it."

"It's your traffic stop," Dailey stated.

I told him, "You found the straw. You make the arrest, and do *not* ask me for a statement or subpoena me."

I had no plans to charge either of them, but I wasn't going to give Double-O-Dick-Dailey that opportunity, nor the opportunity to report me. I decided to postpone my arrest. *I'll fix you.* I thought.

I focused my attention on Jordan, "Contact me in a couple of days to set up a meeting at the police department," I said. "If you don't call, I will issue warrants for you both, understand?"

Officer Dailey stayed with the driver and his passenger until a wrecker driver could be dispatched. I left to locate the white Durango. As I approached West Boiling Springs Lakes Road, Brittany called again.

"I can't talk right now," I told her. "I'm looking for a Durango on West Boiling Springs Lakes."

She started laughing and said to someone else, "He's looking for us."

"You guys are in the Durango?" I asked.

"Yeah." She replied.

"Who's driving?"

"Me."

"What?" I shouted, and then said, "You can't do that. Take it back now."

"You're not mad are you?" Brittany asked. I heard another female voice shout, "We want you to come arrest us!"

"That's not funny," I said. "Who was that?"

"That was Jee." Brittany replied.

"I ain't mad, but you can't just tell me you're doing that," I said. "Whose Durango is it?"

"My dad's, but we're home now."

"Brittany, please don't do that anymore," I said. "If something would've happened, there's a record you've called me, and how would I explain that?"

After we hung up, I called dispatch and reported that I was unable to locate the Durango. I drove around the dirt road a few times so whoever had called about seeing the Durango would see me patrolling the area. "Damn it, Brittany." I said to nobody.

I didn't like the position that she had just put me in.

Two days later, Jordan and his girlfriend set up a meeting at the PD. We met just minutes after I came on duty. We went into the detective's office where I closed the door behind us. I asked them a few questions about the straw, and they both offered to submit to a drug test. I requested a written statement and just as I had hoped, they stated they thought Officer Dailey planted the straw. I told them that I would contact the DA and then them after I decided what was best to do.

After they left, I thought about how it would destroy their futures if I proceeded with the DA on this matter. I already knew in my heart that Dailey had planted that straw.

I bagged up their statements and the coke straw. I drove out West Boiling Springs Lakes Road about three miles to the power lines. I dug a small hole in the sand and dropped the bag in it. I smoked at the time and kept a Zippo lighter attached to my utility belt. I took lighter fluid I'd saved and poured it all over the bag. I lit a cigarette and then the bag. I leaned against my SUV and was feeling like a king as I watched all the evidence go up in flames. I felt like I had the power to erase history - like it never happened. I kicked the bag around some and then poured more fluid on it. I tried to image how pissed off Dailey would get when he found out.

"Fuck him." I said, as I kicked the sand around and then covered the ashes up.

●

Since that incident with Jordan and Dailey "finding" the coke straw, some individuals have since said that I should've let the District Attorney sort it out, but I just followed my heart. I don't regret the choice I made that day. The straw wasn't there when I searched. So once again, I give no apologies for my actions. Dailey planted that straw—it's that simple. And judging from what happened to me soon afterward, it was for the better for both Jordan and his passenger, because there's no telling what would have happened to either of them if charges had been brought.

CAN YOU SEE THE BRUISES

I often patrolled Hwy 87 and stopped at Kopp's Quik Stop. Brittany lived with her father right behind the store. As I started my shift one night the following week, I stopped at Kopp's Quik Stop for my usual cancer sticks, soda, and gum. Moments later, Brittany walked in.

"I have been trying to call you," she explained.

"I know but I've been busy," I said.

"I need to talk to you," she said.

"Give me a minute, and then walk with me to my patrol car."

After I paid for my stuff, Brittany grabbed my arm and escorted me out. "What's going on?" I asked.

"It's my mom and dad again," Brittany said. "All they do is fight about me. Lou won't keep his hands off me. I'm just tired of all this shit. I can't handle it anymore."

"Who is Lou, and what do you mean by that?" I asked.

"He's my mom's boyfriend, and he hits me." She pulled up her sleeve and said, "You can still see the bruise."

I recalled a previous conversation with Buddy, and I didn't see a bruise, so I asked, "Does he hit you with a fist or is he disciplining you and you don't like it."

"Why are you acting like that?" She asked.

"Because I have to know what happened," I replied. "Are you being abused or disciplined?"

Brittany spotted her dad coming home from work, and quickly said, "I gotta go. I'm not supposed to be out of the house." She turned and ran behind the store and disappeared into the woods.

Now I was suspicious. I flagged her dad over and asked him a few questions.

"Brittany tells me that Lou hit her, and I'm trying to figure out if it was abuse or discipline."

"Discipline!" Johnny said rather abruptly. "Brittany does and says things to get attention from anyone she can. If her mouth is open, she's lying." He paused a few seconds before he asked, "Are you going to be around?"

"Yes, till three am." Johnny nodded and then pulled away.

About an hour later, I drove toward Southport on Hwy 133 when the cell phone rang.

"Officer Stidham?" A man's voice asked.

"Yes."

"Can you meet me and Brittany at the police department?"

"I'll be there in about fifteen minutes."

When I arrived, Brittany stood crying. Both Lou and Johnny were with her. Both of them looked angry. Johnny leaned against a post, and Lou was standing with Brittany. "Officer Stidham, Brittany has something to say that I think will clear this whole thing up," Johnny explained.

"I made it up." Brittany said.

I noticed Brittany's wrists were covered in homemade bandages, so I asked what she'd done.

Brittany ripped the bandages off, and Johnny replied, "To get attention."

Lou never spoke. He just walked off. *Awkward!* I thought feeling a little uneasy about Lou's demeanor. Johnny went on to explain that Brittany had caused him and her mother a lot of problems.

He and Brittany left, and as Johnny walked back to his Durango, I wondered whether Brittany had been coached.

As they pulled away, Brittany kept looking back at me. I got the strangest feeling, so strange that the little hairs on the back of my neck stood up. The memories of my own childhood flashed through my head. I thought about how Lou abruptly removed himself from the conversation. I remembered when I was a kid, and just how discouraging it had been for me when I felt like no one believed me.

At the same time, I recalled several conversations I'd had with Buddy about how many times Brittany had been caught lying. I shook it off and went back to what I did best—riding around in my patrol car getting fatter by the mile.

Later that night—

A THREE-WAY

"What are you doing?" Brittany asked.

"Nothing much, just running radar on 87."

"Are you at the golf course?"

"Yeah. Whatcha need? Wait, how'd you know that?"

"I need to show you something."

"Come on Brittany," I said doubting her intentions. "Do you have something to show me for real?"

"I got a black eye from Buddy."

It had been about four hours since I had last seen her and what little I knew of Buddy compelled me to think, *Nope! I don't think so.*

I told her, "I'll meet you at Kopp's at eight o'clock."

"Okay, but don't tell Buddy."

After I hung up, I called Buddy anyway.

"Dude? Check this out, Brittany says you gave her a black eye."

Laughing, Buddy responded, "When did I do this?"

"I guess sometime between 3:30 this afternoon and just now."

"That's impossible. I've been with my dad all evening, and we're at Golden Corral right now."

"I figured as much," I responded. "I just had to ask."

"Wanna do a three way call with her?" he asked. "I'll show you once and for all she's a liar."

"Alright, "I told him, "You call. Tell her I called you and said you had to come in to do a police report."

Buddy called Brittany and clicked me in right before she picked up.

"Hey, what's up baby?" Brittany asked.

"Luke called me. He said you told him I gave you a black eye and now, I have to leave to go do a police report." Buddy said, setting the stage.

"I haven't talked to Luke all day," Brittany responded. "He won't take any of my calls. If he said that he's a damn liar. I didn't say that shit. I'm going to slap him in the face."

"Damn, baby girl," Buddy reacted, "Why you so pissed at Luke?"

"Because he's always taking my dad's side and shit..."

I had heard enough. It was time to crash this party. "I'll take it from here, Buddy." I interrupted. "You are a compulsive liar, Brittany. Why do you do it?"

And with a click she was gone again. "Figures." I responded. Looked like the party was over, or so I thought.

A BROKEN HEART

As if nothing had happened, that following Wednesday when I returned to work, once again, Brittany decided to call. "Can you meet me?" she asked.

I asked what was wrong of course.

"I just really need to talk to you right now," she insisted.

I had gotten in so deep with this free consultation thing that I didn't know where to turn. I told her that I was busy entering a report, but that I would call her when I got done.

"Are you still at the PD?" she asked.

I paused a brief moment, and then felt like a stalked animal hiding from its prey. I told her that I only had about 15 or 20 minutes of paper work left. After we hung up, I went to the restroom and then into the City Hall's kitchen. I poured myself a cup of coffee. Before I could walk back up the hallway, I heard the front door open. "Hello?" came a female's voice. When I got to the end of the hallway, there stood Brittany.

"Damn," I told her, exasperated. "What'd you do, run down here? I told you I'd call."

Brittany's face was red from running and sweat was running down her forehead. "I know, but I needed to talk to you," she said.

She began to tell me that Buddy was being an asshole again, and her dad had just slapped her. She said that she was just so sick of her dad and mother always fighting with her.

"First, why is Buddy being an asshole?" I asked.

"Because we got back together, and he thinks that Bobby and me did it. Now he's broken up with me again," Brittany explained. "I hate him!"

"Okay, you're what 16? Why are you even worried about Buddy? Go get yourself another boyfriend."

"I can't," she replied.

"Yes you can," I said, trying to give good advice. "Don't act like it bothers you one bit. If he calls, speak normal. Don't call him. Don't beg him. Let him come to you."

"What about my dad, though?" Brittany stepped forward and then wrapped her arms around me. She was about to place her head on my chest. I asked, "Why'd he slap you?" I then grabbed her arms and took a step back, all the while thinking, *What was that about?*

"He saw me crying and shit because of Buddy and he was like 'hang up the damn phone, you're not supposed to be talking to him anyway,' so I slammed the door and he came in my room and slapped me across the face."

"He probably felt you disrespected him when you slammed the door," I said, and then I added, "I need to go. I got a call just before you walked in." I quickly slid out the front door attempting to escape. I held it open suggestively nodding my head for her to get a move on.

"Can I go?" She asked as she walked passed.

"No, it's a domestic violence call." I replied. "Seriously, I can't take you with me every time I come on duty. I'll call you later, and we can finish this, okay?"

As she did quite frequently, Brittany threw this in my face, "You said I could call you anytime I felt like hurting myself though."

"I know that, and I meant it, but you call me over some ... simple issues that you can handle yourself." I said. "I'm not trying to be mean, it's just you call me right in the middle of a real call or situation. When I tell you I'm busy, you turn right around, five or ten minutes later, and call back, over and over. You can't keep doing that."

"Fine, you're just like my dad. But what the fuck ever," she said, and started to walk off.

"Brittany?" I called with an authoritative voice. She stopped, turned around and, that time, she had tears in her eyes. I told her, "I am your friend... someone you can come to when you have *real* problems, but you come up here and walk through the parking lot every single time I come on duty. You're calling the police cell when I'm not on duty. Don't you think that is a bit too much?"

Brittany took her "whatever" stance again. Then it suddenly hit me, and I had to ask, "Wait, you're not ... liking me as more than a friend are you?"

"No," she said, "It's just ... I don't know." The tears slowly ran down her cheeks.

"That's sweet," I said softly, but I knew I had to end this right away. She was already crying, and I felt horrible for being the cause. I softened my approach a little, "Look, you're a sweetheart, you really are. You're a very pretty young lady, but I'm a friend, and nothing more, okay?"

I tried to add a little humor to the situation, telling her, "Besides, I'm an old fart."

She threw me a little smile and walked back towards her house. Although she seemed to be okay, I would soon learn ... she wasn't.

CHAPTER 8

CHIEF, YOU'RE UNDER ARREST

BSL had a population of around 3900 people, so having a ride along was not unusual, at least for me. It was "Small Town USA" and nearly everyone treated me like family. Through Dailey, I had become better friends with a couple that were his friends as well, Scott Cisco and Danielle Shruggs. This seemed to make him a little more jealous, not to mention vengeful.

On one hot and humid night, Scott and Danielle were on a ride along with me. We stopped by the police department so I could get caught up on my reports. It had been a busy night, and I hadn't heard from Brittany in a couple days.

I saw vehicle lights pulling up in the parking lot, and looking out the window, discovered it was the chief in his personal truck. Moments later, he walked in with a glass of what looked like iced tea. It didn't take long for the room to fill with the smell of alcohol, both on him and in his glass.

"Do you have alcohol in your glass?" I asked looking up from my paperwork.

"What the hell is it to you?" Chief White replied.

"The law," I pointed out.

I then snapped open the buckle to unlock my handcuffs and stood up, telling him, "Turn around and put your hands behind your back, Chief." I smiled and added, "You're under arrest."

Chief White didn't comply. He gave me a blank stare, and then he picked up the telephone and called Officer Dailey.

"Come pick me up. Officer Stidham's orders."

"What do you expect me to do?" I asked the chief. "You're driving and you expect me to do nothing about it? You reek with alcohol! How do I know you're not testing me?"

"Dailey's coming to pick me up. Leave if you don't like it."

"Chief, don't add resisting, okay?" I said. "Put your glass down and turn around. Oh, and as you would say 'That's an order.'"

●

Holy shit fire and save all the matches! To be able to turn his famous "order" phrase around on him felt so damn exhilarating!

●

Scott and Danielle didn't know what to say, what to do, or what to think. They looked on in amazement as I put the chief in handcuffs and sat him down in one of the office chairs. He groaned and moaned a little. I walked back around the counter and sat down, gloating. I had to take whiz so damn bad, but I wasn't finished with the chief nor was I going to miss out on even a second of watching him squirm. What I did next was mean, but I got my point across.

I picked up the telephone and *pretended* to contact dispatch.

"This is eleven seventy-seven. I'm at the PD. I got eleven-seventy, the chief, here in custody for DUI and open container...." I paused several seconds like I was listening to the person on the other end. "I know, right? What a dumb-ass."

Occasionally I glanced up at the chief. He was near panicking, and I was near whizzing my pants. I paused several seconds again and said, "That's *his* problem, but hey, send me a Brunswick County Sheriff supervisor to take custody." The fear in his eyes was so gratifying. (And to think, later on the chief called me "mediocre?")

I hung up, but just couldn't hold it any longer. I took a second set of handcuffs and locked him to his chair. "Don't go anywhere, Chief," I said, laughing as I ran down the hallway.

Officer Dailey pulled up in his patrol car and Chief White said when Dailey walked in, "Take me home before Luke takes me in."

"That's up to Luke," Dailey said, then he looked at me and asked, "Can I just take him home?"

"Hell no," I said, "He's under arrest. He called you; I didn't." I was trying to be a serious smart ass at that point.

"Dude?" Dailey said, "I promise to take him straight home, and he will not come back out tonight. I'll make sure of that."

I leaned back in my chair and looked at the chief. I slowly shook my head a few times like I was debating with myself. But I wasn't debating. I just wanted to scare the chief a bit more. I wanted the chief to realize that his career was now in my hands.

I asked him, "Do you think you're above the law, Chief?"

He never answered. He just looked up at Dailey for assistance and I swear I thought I saw tears in his eyes. "Let me take him home, Luke?" Dailey asked.

I told the chief, "Stand up and turn around." He was shaking like a leaf. His knees nearly buckled in celebration when he heard my cuff keys jingle. Dailey thanked me and they left. The chief never did thank me, though.

Dailey told me later that during the five-minute journey to the chief's house Chief White personally gave him a "hit" order. Dailey reported the chief told him, "I want you to take him to the woods and kick his ass into shape."

Dailey told me he replied, "You know I can't do that. Just find a reason to fire him."

The chief was supposed to have said then, "I tried damn it! I'll get him sooner or later." Dailey said Chief was squirming in his seat. Dailey told me I needed to get my act together. I blew it off like I did with most things.

Scott and Danielle left, and I continued my shift. I drove down Hwy 87 to patrol near the high school. As I was about to come up on Kopp's Quik Stop parking lot, I saw three females walking near the road. I hit my bright lights and discovered Brittany was one of the girls. I pulled over at the top of her road near the stop sign, and she ran up to my passenger door.

"What are you guys doing out this late?" I asked.

"Just walking. Can we go for ride?"

"Who are they?" I asked, nodding at her two friends.

"Jee and Clara. Just friends of mine."

"That'll be fine for about thirty minutes or so but I don't have any ride along forms for them."

I knew that they would sneak out regardless of whether I liked it or not. Hwy 87 is completely dark except for a few brief parking lots with streets lights. I figured if they were with me, at least they would be safe for the time being.

Brittany waved for Jee Holton and Clara Millings to join us. Brittany got in my vehicle up front and the two girls climbed in the back. I patrolled near one of BSL's schools where there had recently been a break in.

After making my rounds, I started running radar as I drove the girls back down Hwy 87. I didn't have permission forms for Jee or Clara to ride, so I ended their tour pretty quickly. I figured fifteen or twenty minutes wouldn't hurt. As I was about to drop them off in front of Brittany's house, she frantically asked me to drive down a little further because her dad would hear my SUV?

"Snuck out again, huh?" I asked.

I stopped about 50 feet from her house. The girls got out, and Brittany asked, "Can I have a hug?" She ran around to my side of the car and then hugged my neck. Before I knew it, she gave me a quick kiss on my cheek again.

"Don't sneak back out tonight." I said. "I'm serious."

"Okay." She turned and ran to catch up with the other girls.

CHAPTER 9

ALIBI

On August 21, 2006 around noon, the chief called me on my *personal* cell phone to ask whether I would cover Dailey's shift that night—a 12-hour shift beginning at 7 p.m. I agreed and went back to sleep until around four o'clock.

I reported to duty at 7 pm and then Scott and Danielle called around 11 o'clock for another ride-along. Scott had just gotten off work and was still in his wrecker, so we met up at Olde Brunswick General Store.

It had been a quiet night for the most part, but shortly after I picked them up, my cell phone rang.

"Hey. Can I go tonight?" Brittany asked.

Scott, Danielle, and I often played jokes on each other. On that night, Danielle sat up front and Scott sat in the back. He had leaned up from the back seat, but just then I jammed on the brakes and Scott dropped his cigarette in his lap.

"Not tonight. I got some friends with me." I told her, as I looked through my rear view mirror at Scott. Danielle then burst out laughing as Scott frantically swatted at the red-hot ashes burning through his denim coveralls. I started laughing myself. Brittany paused several seconds, and then abruptly hung up.

About an hour later, my phone started ringing continuously. The number was blocked and when I answered, no one spoke. I just heard heavy breathing. It rang at least another 30-something times after that. I just figured most of the blocked calls had to be from Brittany.

I had grown tired of no one speaking when I answered, so I sent all further calls to voice mail. This worked for a while until the caller left numerous voicemails of more heavy breathing.

Besides the phone calls, it remained an eventless night. We rode around for a while. I did make a few traffic stops because I was bored to death. We were so bored that we drove to Southport and walked around the waterway. Scott and I then ran back to my SUV and pulled out, leaving Danielle running behind us up on Main Street.

After we goofed off a bit longer, I drove back to the police department where I logged into Police Pak, an incident report database. I filled out a few reports and then drove Scott and Danielle back to his wrecker near 2:30 that morning. By 2:45 am, give or take, I was on my way home for dinner, a mere five minutes away.

As I pulled back onto Fifty Lakes Drive, my phone rang again. Of course, no one spoke and I heard more heavy breathing, but this time, something was different. I heard soft music playing in the background. I said, "I know this is you Brittany." The caller hung up, but I called back.

"Why do you call and not say anything?' I asked. "Do you think that amuses me?"

"It wasn't me." Brittany said.

"Sure it was. I can still hear the same song on the radio."

Brittany paused and then said, "Whatever. Who was that girl you had in your truck?"

That simple question felt so damned invasive, so I replied, "I don't think that's any of your concern. However, she's..." I paused as I heard her hang up.

I got home about 2:55 am. I had forgotten my house key, so Danette had to let me in the house.

I fixed myself a plate for dinner and then Danette and I sat on the couch watching TV. By 3:30 am, she went back to bed, and I fell asleep on the couch moments later. Danette woke me up at five minutes till seven that morning, so I had to hurry back to the police department. Generally, I signed off duty at 7 am sharp. I was about ten minutes late.

CHAPTER 10

LOG BACK IN

Later that same day, I was irritable from lack of sleep when I contacted dispatch to sign on duty at 3 p.m. I was checking my email when the police cell phone rang.

"Hey it's me, whatcha doing?" Brittany asked.

"I'm checking my email, why?"

"Have you heard from Buddy?"

"No, why?"

As I opened my email, I saw Brittany had sent an email requesting that I go see her new pictures. "I got your email," I said.

"Have you tried to open it yet?" She asked.

"Why did you ask me about Buddy?"

"He and I are fighting again," she said. "I thought he would call you."

"Why does your picture keep logging me out?" I asked.

"It does that sometimes. You gotta log back in."

"Yeah. I've done that about a gazillion times now."

I was easily aggravated that day. "It keeps logging me out." I said. "Is it just a picture of my patrol vehicle?"

"It worked. I got it," Brittany said.

"What?" I asked.

"Oh um, nothing," she said. "Delete it, okay?"

"All right."

I had no idea what I'd just falling victim to...

YOU'LL BE SORRY

It was just after mid-night on August 28, 2006. Brittany called and told me that Jee Holton, Clara Millings, and she were riding around in her dad's truck again. I heard one of the other girls shout, "We want you to come arrest us" in the background.

"Why do you think it's okay to tell me this?" I asked.

"Because you're a cool cop," Brittany said. Then she added, "You don't care."

"I don't care?" I asked, feeling like a pushover. "You've put me in a position."

I paused several seconds before continuing, "Look, I was a teenager too. I know you're just having fun but I'm a cop, Brittany. This ain't cool."

"He's mad now," Brittany said sarcastically to the other girls.

Feeling like she had taken advantage of my kindness, I bluntly said, "Take the truck back. Right now! There's record of you calling me. If you get hurt, it's my ass!"

"Fine. What the fuck ever." She replied.

By then, I was more than just a little offended. "Get mad. I don't give a damn." I said. "Tell you what? Take the truck back before I get there because if I find you, I will take you to jail. Do you understand me?"

"I said fine." Brittany said, and then asked, "Are you going to tell my dad?"

"I'm on my way. If I find you, you're history."

I paused several seconds again listening to Brittany tell her friends that I was being an asshole so I interrupted and said,

"We can't be friends anymore if you continue to do this."

She hung up as I heard her say, "He's coming."

I then headed to her area as fast as I could go with lights and siren.

Brittany had already made it back home by the time I rolled past her house. I slowed to a creep with just my blue lights on. One of the girls peaked through window blind before the room went dark.

"Bet that scared ya, huh?" I said.

Nearly three hours would pass before Brittany blocked her number and called again. Meanwhile, I sat in the police department sleeping, while waiting on Officer Dailey to come in for the next shift.

Brittany called a few more times and I just sent her to voicemail. Near 6:30 am, Dailey walked in the PD and woke me up. Brittany called again but I answered then hung up. She called right back.

"Help me," She said sounding to be in a lot of pain.

"What's wrong with you now?" I asked with enormous doubt.

"I've taken a lot of pills and shit. My stomach's on fire."

"Why are you taking pills?"

"I don't want to live anymore."

"Okay, that does it!" I said. "No more Mr. Nice Guy."

I took an oath. And I had an obligation. I was a cop and on duty. I had no choice but to contact the medics. But first, I tried to call her bluff.

"Bullshit, you're not killing yourself," I said. "If you keep this up, you're going to force me to do my job."

"And what's that?" Brittany asked sarcastically.

"My job, Brittany!" I replied. "I will come to your house. Bring the medics. Tell your dad everything, and have you committed."

"No, don't. I'll get in trouble," she pleaded.

"That's the whole idea."

"You do and you'll be sorry," she said. And just like that, she hung up again.

"That's what I thought." I responded.

Moments later, the cell phone rang again. I handed Dailey the cell phone. "It's for you," I said.

When Dailey answered the phone, he said that Brittany spoke in a frantic tone, and said, "Help me!"

Dailey asked who was calling and then he said it was like everything was hunky dory and Brittany asked, "Is Luke there?"

"No he's not," he replied and asked, "Who is this?"

Brittany hung up again.

Dailey called back and told her we knew who she was. "You've forced us to do our job," he said.

Again, she hung up.

"Let's teach her a lesson," Dailey said.

So he contacted the medics and then he and I drove "urgent traffic" to her house. Regardless of whether we believed her or not, we had to treat her call as a suicide threat. When we arrived, Dailey beat on her door repeatedly with his baton. Her father, Johnny, answered the door, and we informed him of Brittany's suicide attempt. Johnny became extremely irate.

We followed him as he stomped down the hallway. He said, "This is just another one of her attention-grabbing stunts backfiring!" He led us to a small bedroom where Brittany laid in bed looking scared to death.

"Did you call them saying that you was gonna to kill yourself?" Johnny shouted.

"I took some pills," she claimed, and then began to cry.

Dailey tapped me on the shoulder and pointed to the walls. Brittany had about 50 pictures of my patrol vehicle plastered everywhere. There were 10 pictures of my house under construction, and about another 50 pictures of Buddy and his fire truck. "What the fuck?" I whispered.

I tapped Johnny on the shoulder and said, "Come with me."

We walked down the hallway to the kitchen where Johnny's girlfriend waited. She was wearing a bathrobe smoking a cigarette.

"Brittany told me that you've molested her in the past," I said to Johnny. He shook his head and said, "She better not start that shit again." He ran his hands threw his stringy hair.

"What do you mean?" I asked.

"She's done this before and got her boyfriend involved," he explained.

"Who's her boyfriend?"

"Well, her ex-boyfriend, Bobby McCorkle."

"I remember that," I replied. "I've read the reports." I leaned against the kitchen doorway with my back to the hall.

"Mr. Lewis? Brittany calls me way too much about nothing at all. Every time I turn around, she's emailing me." I explained. "This has got to stop. Her walls are covered with my pictures. Honestly, that's a little freaky."

"She looks up to you, Officer Stidham, but I'm sorry she's troubled you."

Sarcasm in his tone, he said, "I think she may even have a crush on you." Then he poured himself a cup of coffee.

At that moment, it became extremely clear to me that we were looking and talking at more than a crush. Brittany was obsessed.

Meanwhile, the medics had already arrived and had been in Brittany's bedroom a few moments. About 10 minutes later, they walked her out. My back was still to the hallway when Brittany leaned in towards me and whispered, "You'll be sorry."

I would later find out—Brittany made good on her threat.

SINISTER E-MAILS

Almost two weeks had passed when Officer Felts was on duty when I came in one day. He leaned against the front door as I prepared the paperwork for my shift.

"Here comes yur girlfriend again," he said. "This bout the third time she done walked through the lot."

"She's not my girlfriend," I said. "Where's she at?"

"Over yonder walking dis way."

"If she comes in, tell her I'm out on a call," I said. I grabbed my clipboard and hurried down the hallway to the City Hall.

Moment later, Felts yelled, "She done gone."

I sat down at the officer's desk checking my emails and noticed an unusual amount of them from Brittany. I opened a new message from her that was out of the ordinary. She had written the email in such a way that it was a little inappropriate. She asked me to fill out a questionnaire about my likes and dislikes about her. It was a rating survey, each answer on a scale of one to ten, with ten being the highest.

I replied, without choosing any numbers, asking whether she had sent me this by mistake, and to please be more careful. Brittany replied that it wasn't her, that it was her friends sending me the emails. Later that evening, I received another fill in the blank email. One word would be missing in a sentence type of thing. There was one question that read, "I want to 'blank' you." The 'blank' was nothing more than an underscore in the sentence. I was supposed to fill in the missing word.

In the reply, I told her that either she or one of her friends emailed me this thing again, and suggested that she make sure that I wasn't made part of a mailing list. I never got a response back. I began deleting the emails and then sent Brittany an email asking, "Are you sending me these emails on purpose?" Again, she never responded, and she wasn't calling either.

Over the next several days, at random, when I tried to login to my email account, it reported my account was already in use. "What the hell?" I said. It never dawned on me what was really going on.

Around that same time, Brittany started showing up at the police department every time I came on duty. She never stopped, but kept walking through the parking lot like she was going to the playground nearby. I felt like a stalked animal again.

I called in several times and told the chief that I would be a few minutes late. I was hoping to miss her but that never seemed to work.

She waited on me from the playground. I would cringe, as I was about to turn into the police department's parking lot.

"Holy Shit!" I would say. "And there she is."

I watched as she stalked me with her eyes. She seemed so damned evil looking across her eyebrows.

Sometimes she would leave when I walked in the police department; other times, she waited until I left again on patrol.

Either I, or one of the other people from the PD who often drove my SUV, left the doors of my SUV unlocked a few times. Brittany emailed me a picture of her in the back seat with a message that read, "You left your doors unlocked dumb-dumb."

The image of the shadow of the person taking the picture appeared to be another female.

She then called repeatedly with her number blocked again. She would never speak, and sometimes just hung up. When I called Brittany back, and she answered, she blamed dialing on her pocket book or this baby that she had started watching. She rang my police cell 20 or more times in less than 30 minutes on several occasions.

This was all getting way out of hand.

Finally, I wrote her an email, a nice one, and explained that she had the wrong idea about me. I wrote that she should not let her friends write me emails, pretending to be her. I wrote to stop calling so much. I thought I had handled it as peacefully as I knew how under the circumstance.

SINISTER TELEPHONE CALL

A few days later, on September 13, 2006, it was late evening and I hung out at the police department editing Officer's Dailey reports. The caller ID displayed a number that I didn't recognize.

"Hey. It's Brittany," she said. "What are you doing?

"Nothing," I replied. "How you doing?"

"I'm doing better, not great, but you know."

"Right," I said. "Life ain't better huh?"

"No. It's not great at all. It sucks. Nothing getting better. You know, whatever," she replied "I talked to Buddy though."

"Did you?" I asked.

"Yeah."

"You know um, your folks are not gonna let you hang around the fire department or anybody like that anymore." I said.

"Why?"

"That's what I heard," I replied.

"Who you hear that from?"

"Um, somebody, I think your dad."

"My dad hasn't said anything."

"They searched your phone records and they've seen where you been calling me too," I said.

"What does that mean?"

"Um, they just made the comment they thought you had something going on with me."

"But he don't know ..." she paused before continuing, "anything, right?"

"Right." I replied, thinking she was referring to her sneaking out. It didn't hit me until much later what she really meant.

"Are you by yourself right now?" she asked.

"Sorta," I replied.

"I went to the hospital, right?" she asked.

"Yep."

"You know that they give you the whole, every test you can think of?"

"Yeah."

"They gave me a drug test."

"Right."

"They found Valium in my system."

"Damn!" I replied.

"Yeah," Brittany said laughing.

"How?" I asked, "Where were you taking Valium?" I was shocked by her comment because she had never told me about any Valiums, but then again, why would she?

"Where'd I get them?" she asked.

"No," I replied. "Where have you been taking them?"

"I took them that night."

"Wow. Better stay off that crap."

"I'm not going to do that anymore. I told you that," she said. "Well I didn't tell you that, but I'm just under a lot of stress."

"Yeah." I responded. I was only half-heartedly into her conversation because I was busy reading emails.

"Thanks to you," she then said.

"What do you mean, thanks to me?" I asked. I leaned back waiting for her answer.

"I don't think you really want me to say that."

She paused for a second so I interrupted, "Go ahead and say it."

"You," she replied.

"How do I put you under stress?"

"You know how."

"No I don't," I replied, and it still hadn't hit me yet what she meant.

"You are like most guys," she then said. "You got what you wanted and that's it."

And that's when it hit me.

"Did you or did you not?" she asked.

"Don't even hand me that," I replied in my smart-ass and somewhat loud tone.

"Did you?" Brittany asked.

"I don't know what you're talking about." I replied.

"You got what you wanted and then stopped talking to me." Brittany replied.

"No I did not." I replied.

"Yeah, you did because that was what half of my problem. You," she said. "That hurts you know. That's not fair to me."

"I don't know what to tell you Brittany. I mean um, that didn't happen. We've never had sex."

"Whatever." Brittany said and then she was silent for several seconds. "But whenever you're by yourself, call me back."

"I'm by myself!" I replied as I raised my voice again.

"No," she said. "Um, when you're not at the PD at all."

Brittany went silent again for several seconds, and then I heard mumbling in the background. I made out Brittany responding with, "I don't know" in a sad tone of voice.

"Hello?" I said.

"Huh?" Brittany asked.

"What'd you say?"

"I said I do need to talk to you about some stuff."

"Then talk to me!"

"No!" Brittany suddenly said in a quick and panicked loud voice. I thought that she was talking to the baby she had been watching—I was wrong. Dead wrong.

"It's a little problem. A little." Brittany said.

"Like what?"

"Answer me this, you told me you had surgery, you lying to me?"

"No. Why?" I asked, thinking that was an odd question.

"You're dead serious?"

"Yeah."

"Are you one hundred percent positive?" Brittany asked.

"I'm one hundred percent positive. Why..." I asked, and was about to ask why she was asking that question when she interrupted and replied, "I haven't got my period."

"Might wanna talk to Buddy then." I replied laughing. "Why are you telling me this?" I added.

"How are you going to blame it on Buddy?" she asked.

"You told me you and Buddy did it for three weeks or something like that."

"Yeah, we did, but you came after him."

I went silent a few seconds thinking, *Is this a joke?* "Uh, huh," I said, as if I were searching for her agenda.

"It was just you," she said. "What am I supposed to do?"

"Brittany, I'm, look, I don't know what you are supposed to do," I replied.

"Ok, whatever." she said "That's fine."

"I mean, if it wasn't Buddy, who else was it?" I asked. "I don't know what to tell you. It wasn't me."

"Not 'cause you had that surgery thing?" Brittany asked.

"Do what?" I asked. I was just so thrown back by what she was asking that I thought *what the fuck are you doing?*

"I said not..."

"Look." I said interrupting again. "On a serious note, as far as you being pregnant? I don't know what you're trying to get me to say, Brittany. It wasn't me!"

"That's fine. I was just telling you." Brittany said. Then in a sad tone she said, "Whatever. Just call me later. All right? Bye."

CHAPTER 11

SHADOW FIGURES

Later that night, after a few hours of routine patrol, I drove to Police Lieutenant Ledbetter's house for lunch near 10 o'clock. Lt. Curtis Ledbetter, divorced, lived just off the west end of East Boiling Spring Road. He had rented a room from his high school friend, Ted Patrick. A silver-headed Casanova wanna-be, Lt. Ledbetter thought himself a lady's man. Like Lt. Ledbetter, Ted loved to party. The two held cookouts nearly every weekend—Lots of women, alcohol, and loud music. That night was no exception.

My normal work schedule started at 3 o'clock in the afternoon and lasted for the next 12 hours. I had made it a habit of taking my lunch about midway through my shift, and decided to go to the lieutenant's house to eat that day.

Dailey was also on duty that night until 7 the following morning, and when I arrived, was already there. Inspecting Dailey as I walked in, I saw him lower a salt-rimmed glass from his mouth.

"Dailey, are you drinking?" I asked.

This was a boisterous, cigarette smoking and beer-drinking crowd with the waft of unbathed bodies and Mötley Crüe's *Girls, Girls, Girls,* crackling through the speakers of an old boom box.

"I took something for my headache and chased it with her Margarita." Dailey said. He pointed to a redheaded stripper dancing on a coffee table.

A freckled, slender woman, Margarita was nearly naked. She wore a pink thong that was so tight it appeared to slice through her hips. Her blue-veined breasts ballooned and fell like quivering jellyfish as she pranced around. The floor was strewn with clothes, and the top of the kitchen table was crowded with beer bottles, dirty glasses, and half-eaten plates of spaghetti. I became lost in the foul smell of smoke, whiskey, and something that smelled of rotten tuna in an old shoebox.

The Lieutenant was a plain-clothes officer. Sometimes he called himself "Detective," other times he was the "Lieutenant." On this night, he kicked back in the kitchen doing nothing. His large belly rubbed against the table.

"You want some leftovers, Luke?" He asked, after taking a long draw from his cigar. Ted was busy in the bathroom with a prostitute he later found out had full blown AIDS.

"My god it stinks in here," I said wrinkling my nose like someone just cut a ripe, wet, bubbling, chocolate-colored fart. "What's that smell?"

Stepping over the mounds of clothes and making my way to the kitchen, I spotted a ribbed condom carelessly discarded on an already over-flowing wastebasket. Used napkins, dirty paper plates, and several plastic forks were scattered on the floor.

"On second thought ... don't answer that" I said.

I walked back out the front door, across the porch and down the steps when the chief telephoned me back to the police department. "So much for lunch." I said.

Pulling into the parking lot, I noticed several vehicles that I hadn't seen before. As I walked up the sidewalk, I looked through the windows and the glass door, and that's when I noticed that the front room was empty. I opened the door and walked around the front counter listening for any movement down the hallway. Strangely, the light was on in the reception area and the front door was unlocked. The chief's door was also cracked open, but his office was pitch black. This was unusual behavior for the chief because he was adamant about turning out the lights and locking all the doors.

"Chief?" I called.

The room still carried the smell of new paint. The chief had persuaded the City Manager into a new scheme of Gun Metal gray and Sky Mist blue. The once outdoor carpet covered concrete floor now bore a painted checker board design. An oil painting of the chief hung on the wall just behind the counter. His eyes seemed to follow anyone who entered by the front door. It was a rather small police department. Behind the "L" shaped counter was hardly enough room for two officers to pass. It had been positioned to force a left-hand turn upon entering.

From the cover of the darkness, the chief sprung from his office. "I gotta take your gun." He said holding out his hand.

"What?" I asked, startled by his sudden appearance. My birthday was just a week prior, so I expected a practical joke any day. Unsure of his purpose, I stared at the chief inspecting his facial expression. I never cared much for the chief, nor did I trust him. For a split second I hoped the chief was ready to end our indifference.

"I gotta take your gun!" Chief White said sternly.

I was reaching for my side arm when a shadowy figure rushed me from behind. He grabbed my gun, and it startled me, so I jerked away to protect myself.

A second shadowy figure leaped from behind the chief with a gun to my face. "Don't move, "he said.

The first shadowed figure twisted my gun wrist behind my back. I went into fight mode because neither of the gunmen had identified themselves. I saw no badges, no IDs, nothing that would have led me to believe they were law enforcement officers. The first gunman then grabbed a handful of my hair and then slammed my head down on Allison's desk. I was able to turn my face just in time to avoid a busted nose.

SPECIAL AGENT GHENT

Charles L. Ghent, the first shadowed figured, was a Special Agent for the North Carolina State Bureau of Investigation. Ghent was promoted to detective with the Mt. Pleasant, South Carolina Police Department where he served two years in the narcotics division. After two prior denials, the State Bureau of Investigation finally agreed to interview him.

The second gunman, Special Agent Eugene Wesley, was hired shortly after Ghent. New to the game, he looked at Agent Ghent as a mentor.

"I guess I kind of was a little afraid of him sometimes," Wesley admitted in an interview with the state's Attorney General's office.

Agent Wesley, a towering 24-year-old Scottish-American had a large chest and arms to match. It wasn't that he was afraid of Ghent; it was just Wesley was afraid of what Ghent would do. "He takes it to the limit," he said.

Agent Wesley, fresh out of rookie school, made a living as a pizza delivery boy while he attended college at UNC of Wilmington. He met Ghent one summer night when he was near the college on a pizza delivery run. "He ordered two large cheese pizzas," he said.

Agent Ghent was decked out in full body armor when he opened the door. Wesley immediately enlisted with the State Bureau of Investigation. Two months later, he was an SBI agent-in-training.

Ghent never lost his poise. A master craftsman of his trade, he never showed a trace of emotion. Ghent was known by the local officers to be a machine. He was the underdog that stockpiled fear in his suspect with a mixture of wicked interpretations and unscientific experiments precisely calculated to produce the result he sought. If Ghent was out to make an arrest, he stalked his prey like a wooded animal. He was an expert at setting traps and manipulating his victim's path. No officer dared to confront him, for fear of retaliation.

With my head pressed against Allison's desk, Agent Ghent bent my arm behind my back, and shouted "SBI! You're under arrest!"

"Why didn't you say that before you broke my wrist?" I replied.

Ghent instructed me to place both my hands on top of my head. I complied and he and Wesley then tried to remove my police utility belt. Ghent reached around me from behind and unbuckled my first belt—the one that held all my police gadgets. Ghent then acted confused as to why it doesn't come off.

I look down at his hands as he pulled on my utility belt and started to laugh. "You have to unsnap the belt keepers." I said.

"What's that?" Wesley asked.

I was stunned. I didn't know what to say, so I reached down behind my back with my left hand, grabbed one of my many belt keeps, and pulled it loose.

"This is a belt keeper. It holds the utility belt to my pants belt." I said. "You guys are SBI and don't know that?"

I guess Ghent figured that I had just disrespected him, because he grabbed a hand full of my hair and slammed my head down on Allison's desk again. The chief started to speak up, "That's not ne...", but he went silent again.

"I told you not to move," Ghent said.

He dug his elbow into my temple. He then cuffed my hands behind my back and then raised them high in the air. I had to stand on my tiptoes to avoid him breaking my arms. He was taking his brutality a little too far, and I was starting to get pissed—not a good thing.

"You don't have to be so damn mean!" I shouted.

At first, my voice was calm, but ended nearly yelling, and by then, I jerked around. I was being pushed into fight mode. About that time Sheriff Ronald Hewitt walked in the front door holding a shotgun.

"Everything all right?" he asked.

"Piece of cake," Ghent replied.

Ghent led me to the front reception area where I took a seat. He then took my keys and asked where my locker was. I told him and then Ghent asked, "I'm not going to find any child porn in there, am I?"

"What the fuck do you mean by that?" I asked, extremely insulted.

Agent Wesley stayed behind and he asked whether I knew Brittany Lewis. I said yes, that I knew her through the neighborhood. "You've been arrested for engaging in sexual intercourse with her," Wesley said.

"What?" I asked surprised. "What the hell are you talking about? When did this happen?"

Wesley took a second before he responded. "I can already see you're going to do this the hard way."

"Dude? You do know that I committed her for a suicide attempt, right?" I asked.

"Yes. And you're the blame for that." He replied.

"Says who? Brittany," I asked.

"She said that you used her for sex."

"Brittany?" I asked. Wesley nodded his head yes. Then I recalled my telephone conversation with Brittany earlier that day.

"Don't you see this is revenge?" I asked, but my words made no difference. The damage had been done. I knew, by the next day, the news of my arrest would be headlines across the east coast of North Carolina. I would be branded as a monster.

Agent Ghent and Wesley grabbed me up by my arms, rushed me out the front door and across the parking lot toward Ghent's unmarked police vehicle. I stumbled trying to keep up. At times, my feet dragged across the pavement. "Slow down," I said. "You're dragging me."

As we reached his car, agent Ghent slammed my head against the trunk, "Is that any better asshole," he asked. It felt like he was trying to push my head through the trunk lid.

Agent Wesley opened the front passenger's door, "Just put 'em in man, and let's go."

Sheriff Ronald Hewitt walked back up and he and Agent Wesley got in the back seat. Ghent drove us to the Brunswick County jail.

After we arrived at the jail, Agent Ghent stood waiting for the door to be buzzed open. His hand pressed against my back forcing me tightly against the wall. Sheriff Hewitt contacted dispatch and gave the order to buzz us in. The door buzzed open and with a slap to the back, Ghent clutched my police uniform in a fist.

"Let's go, pretty boy," he said.

Agent Ghent led me through the door displaying his hard-earned work with a smile. He then led me near the counter where I still forced a smile when I stepped up to be booked. The jailers, consisting mostly of my rookie graduating class, looked on in awe at my horrifying appearance.

A small trail of blood ran down from my head where Ghent had slammed it against either Allison's desk or his trunk, or both.

"It only hurts when I laugh," I said with a chuckle.

INTERROGATION

I was still in police uniform, handcuffed, and shackled, when Ghent escorted me into an interrogation room. "Have a seat," he said.

Agent Ghent and I sat facing each other. I had interviewed for a position at the Sheriff's office in the same room myself, so I knew that a hidden clock camera was placed behind Ghent. I sat facing the camera.

As Ghent sat down, he grabbed the bottom of his chair and slid in close. I reacted, holding my hand out as a stop sign, and then slid my chair back.

"Don't do that," I said.

Ghent attacked again, but this time when he moved his chair in his knees catapulted into mine.

Believing the whole event would be recorded; I ignored Ghent's first assault. "I have the emails between you and Brittany." Ghent continued, "They confirm everything she said happened."

He laid printed copies of the emails down in front of me and said, "Brittany said that the two of you had sex, that you fingered her, and that you kissed her twice."

I said, "None of that bullshit is true and my days of finger banging precious in her pretty pink panties disappeared way back in my early twenties."

I again slid my chair back and said to Ghent, "You mean to tell me that you ended my career on emails from a suicidal juvenile? That I committed? You took her word over mine?"

"Just admit it, Ghent said. "You know you fucked her." He grabbed the bottom of his chair and slid his knees into my knees yet again.

"Don't do that!" I shouted. "I know what you're doing." I slid my chair back against the wall.

"If you'll just say you fucked her, I'll tell the judge you thought she was sixteen," Ghent said, and for the third time and much harder, rammed himself into my knees.

"Ghent? You do that again, I promise you, I'll mess you up." I said.

Within seconds, Ghent's assistant investigating officer, Detective Simpson burst in the room. "Is everything okay in here?" she asked. Ghent nodded his head yes and told me to look over the emails. "Tell me what happened," he said.

"Now that you have a camera on your back, you ain't so tough now are ya?" I asked, as I smiled and pointed to the camera. I picked up several of the emails, glanced them over, and then separated them into two piles.

"I didn't write these emails," I said, pointing to the first pile. "I wrote some of these, but I didn't say all this shit to her," I said pointing to the second pile

"Is that not you in those emails?" Ghent asked.

"Yeah. But I didn't say this. Where did you get these?"

"I got them from Brittany."

"Of course you did. Give me a computer, and I'll show you that ain't in my emails."

Agent Ghent left the room only to return moments later with a laptop. "Here," he said. "It's all set up for you." He handed me his laptop.

I opened the Internet and typed in the MySpace web-site address. After the screen finished loading, I typed in my user-name and password. I opened my Inbox folder and then opened the same email Ghent had. "I told you." I said. "So how do you have that when mine states this?" I turned the laptop around for Ghent to compare.

Ghent returned to my Inbox folder and asked, "Where are all your other emails?"

"I don't keep emails long. I delete the most useless, just like most red blooded Americans," I replied. "That's none of your business anyway." I turned the laptop back around and closed out my account.

"You know you fucked her," Ghent said.

"I didn't have sex with Brittany, nor anything else she said I did." I responded "She has kissed me on the cheek." I pointed to my left cheek. "That's it, and that's not illegal."

Ghent leaned back in his seat and said, "You're going to make me do this the hard way aren't you?"

I leaned my head against the wall thinking *I can't believe this is happening.*

"You're not going to sit here and accuse me anymore." I said. "That's it. Stop."

Ghent stood up. "Let's take a break," he said. "We'll continue when we get back."

I knew that no matter what I said, Ghent wasn't going to believe me. He was more concerned about convicting me, rather than accepting the possibility that Brittany had played him as well. But then again, when considering what I discovered some three or four years later from the local newspapers, better explained how some of the agents with the North Carolina State Bureau of

Investigation had resorted to altering case reports and conducting unscientific experiments to bolster a prosecutor's case. I just had no idea how far Ghent would go to get his conviction.

SEARCH WARRANT

Meanwhile, it was just after midnight, and Danette explained that she was awoken by a knock at the front door. She suspected that I had forgotten the house keys again. She opened the front door staying out of view because she had on only a tank top and panties. When I didn't enter, she peeked around the door to find Brunswick County Sheriff's Detective Lori Simm and Deputy Brian Hutler standing on the porch. Fearing the worst had happened to me, she gasped for air. "Oh my God," she said. "What's wrong? Where's my husband?"

"Mrs. Stidham, we have a search warrant. Your husband's in custody." Detective Simms said. "He's been charged with statutory rape and sex offenses, and two counts of taking indecent liberties with a child."

"What?" she asked. "You're kidding, right?"

"I wish she was." Deputy Hutler replied.

"He's been communicating with a 14-year-old girl on MySpace. I have a copy of the emails here if you would like to see them," Detective Simms said.

Deputy Hutler and Danette sat at the kitchen table looking through the emails. "My husband would never do this with an underage girl," Danette said. "Someone has made a terrible mistake. I know my husband."

Detective Simms went through each room, flipping on the lights, waking Nathan, our 10-year-old son, and taking pictures. She searched through boxes, dresser drawers, and under beds. Simms seized our son's computer and a small box of computer parts.

"Why is she the only one searching?" Danette asked Deputy Hutler.

"I'm sorry," he replied, and he dropped his head. "I've known Luke for a while, and I just don't think..."

"I'm done," Simms interrupted, as she walked into the kitchen.

"How can you be so sure just from these emails?" Danette asked. "They don't even look right."

"Mrs. Stidham, we don't arrest our own kind unless we have something," Simms replied.

Deputy Hutler followed Simms out the front door, but stepped back to stick his head in the door. He whispered to Danette, "Tell Luke I've got nothing to do with this." Danette said Hutler frowned rather gently as he lowered his head again to leave.

●

Still shackled, I inched my way to the sally port with leg irons chained to my waist belt. As Ghent and I were smoking, Agent Wesley was scanning my patrol vehicle for DNA traces.

"Your truck lights up like a Christmas tree." Agent Wesley said.

I shook my head disgusted and said, "A hand print will show up as DNA. It's my patrol vehicle, and I've had several people in the back seat, genius."

Detective Simpson then joined us. "I thought you two were about to fight in there," she said.

"We were," I replied.

Agent Ghent placed his hand on my shoulder. "You ready to head back?"

"For what?" I asked. "More questions?"

"We discussed this," he replied.

"I ain't saying shit. Process me. I got what I wanted." I said, as I blew smoke from my lips.

Ghent slapped me on the shoulder. "You got it, smart ass."

●

I waited on a bench just inside the processing area where numerous times before I had requested my own prisoners to have a seat.

Brunswick County Magistrate R. D. Todd came out from his office. He was smiling and had left Agent Ghent behind.

"Your bond is three-hundred-thousand-dollars, secured." Todd said.

"Are you serious?" I asked. "Three-hundred-thousand-dollars?"

"Shit happens" Todd said, as he got up and walked away.

"Good job, Todd!" I yelled down the hallway. "Damn good job!"

Chief White and Officer Dailey strode into the booking area about that time. "Here, you're suspended pending the outcome of your case," the chief said and then handed me a sealed letter.

"Yeah, I know. That's kind of a given." I folded the letter and placed it in my front pocket. Then I continued, "Oh, Chief. I am going to need a copy of Brittany's ride-along approval form."

Chief White paused a few seconds before answering, "I don't know what you're talking about."

What the fuck? I thought, and then said, "Yes you do. I gave it to you."

I got that sickening feeling in my stomach right then. The chief responded by shaking his head. "Let's go Dailey," he said.

Dailey drove the chief back to the BSL Police Department where the chief had parked his personal truck.

What Chief White chose to do next was highly illegal because evidence does not just up and disappear on its own.

CHAPTER 12

BOND HEARING

I had gotten word to a local attorney, Adrian Anderson, and requested that he represent me at my bond hearing. The next morning, I was escorted to the courtroom wearing only a white T-shirt and orange sweat pants. Adrian stood at the defendant's table waiting. The leg iron chains I was locked in were so short that I fell on the floor every other step. My hands were cuffed to my waist belt so I was unable to catch myself to avoid falling. I hit the ground hard several times. I could tell the deputy behind me wanted to help, but something or someone prevented him. I assumed he was afraid of being accused of showing favoritism.

I felt so humiliated. Brittany's mother and father grinned every time I fell. I watched as my brother glared Johnny's smile back down his throat with his own vicious look. Danette, my mother, and my sisters cried in horror and shock at my appearance.

"Your honor, we have Luther Luke D. Stidham up for a bond hearing, the prosecuting attorney Tiffany Campbell said, and then added, "He is making a request that his bond be lowered. The State objects on that request."

"Objection entered. You may proceed." Judge Barefoot said.

"Mr. Stidham lured the victim, Brittany Lewis, a minor female out using email messages through MySpace where, after he earned her trust, he physically raped her in his official patrol SUV. Obviously, he is a flight risk and a danger to society. For these reasons, the State objects to a lower bond."

"Does the defense want to be heard?" Judge Barefoot asked.

"I am not aware of any implied force. That's the first I've heard about it," Adrian said.

"That's the information that I have at this time." Tiffany replied.

"I'll cut it in half. That's the best I can do." Judge Barefoot replied.

I forced a smile again as I looked at my family. This whole thing was just like a horrible, surreal nightmare. This was the first time I had heard that Brittany had accused me of forcible rape. I turned away, humiliated, then stood up and inched my way back behind closed doors.

CHAPTER 13

DRUG RAID

I remained in jail 13 days and was segregated from all the other inmates while I waited for my uncle to post my bond. Meanwhile, I was a nervous wreck. As the other inmates passed my door, they would open the peep hole and flip me off or beat on my door at all hours during the day and night. Every time my door opened, I stood back against the wall, waiting, ready, and positive I was about to be rushed.

I was mostly fed brown bagged lunches with an apple, with the exception of breakfast. Before one meal, after I opened my bag and found that someone had spit on my food, I didn't eat for about two days. By dinner the second day, I was starving and hypoglycemic, so I had to eat something. I picked through my food carefully. There was always something.... snot smashed into my sandwich, a bite taken out from my apple, or something floating in the tea. My breakfast tray had been snapped open on several occasions, so I usually put it to the side.

Eventually, I sat peeping through the tray door as they rolled up with the food dolly. If my tray of bagged lunch was picked at random, I ate. If it wasn't, I didn't. This one kid, whom I had never met, slipped a second bag through my door after I watched this bald-headed, beer-bellied, scruffy looking inmate grab my bagged lunch from his back pocket. I thought I might have arrested the beer-belly guy once or twice for domestic violence.

The kid and the beer-bellied inmate exchanged a few obscene words as they rolled the food cart down the hallway. Maybe it was a trick. Maybe they had caught on to my stealth operation, but I didn't care much that day. My sugar had dropped so low by then that I barely had enough strength to even eat. I sat on the floor, my whole body trembling, as I forced food into my mouth until it was full. I was even too weak to chew. I just gagged and swallowed what I could; positive it would all come back up again anyway. It was amazing how hunger drove me to eat what I felt sure was tainted food.

When Danette first came to visit me, we had to sit in different rooms with a monitor and camera. My monitor was in C Dorm, and moments after I entered the room, a deputy had to stand guard beside me. The other inmates were walking up behind me, flexing or flipping me off again. One guy just brushed the back of my head as he imitated smacking me. I watched them more than I looked at my wife.

It got so bad that every time I was moved to shower or for processing, the jail was put on lock down. All the other inmates stood at the doorways and windows, glaring and talking smack.

"Fuck you, pig!" a voice called out from one of the cells.

"How does it feel you, son-of-a-bitch?" another voice shouted.

"I'ma get cha Stidham," a too-familiar voice said. That voice and those words shook my core because I feared that late night attack under the cover of darkness.

I was extremely afraid for my safety. I would have done or said anything to get out of there. I felt like an unarmed cop in a roomful of vengeful assholes I had arrested, which is essentially what I was.

I looked up and recognized this guy as Kevin Green. Kevin was a known crack dealer. Dailey had obtained a search warrant for Kevin's house in June 2006 and I assisted in executing it. Five BSL officers served the warrant. I was the last officer to enter the house. The house turned up clean, therefore, I had questioned Dailey whether he had just served a "grudge warrant." Dailey often spoke ill-mannered words about Kevin, and often stated that he was a "nigger dating a white chick." In my opinion, Officer Dailey was a racist and I had heard him call Kevin's girlfriend "a skunk" or "zebra" because she dated Kevin.

Kevin hadn't been at home during the search. Angie, Kevin's girlfriend, and their son, Daren, were alone in the house. Angie had just gotten out of the shower and was caught totally by surprise when the door was kicked in and officers entered. The chief, Ledbetter, and another officer entered the front door. Dailey and I entered by the back.

"Put your hands in the air!" Dailey shouted, as he ran into Kevin's bedroom. I entered the bathroom and then laundry room. Daren, in his bedroom on the opposite side of their mobile home, continued playing, unaware of the events unfolding in the other side of the house.

"I don't have any clothes on." Angie had said, trying to cover herself somehow.

"Keep your hands up and don't move," Dailey ordered. "Do you have anything on you," he asked.

"I'm nude. Where am I supposed to put it?" Angie said.

Chief White and the other officers were in the kitchen and had cleared the rest of the house. I entered the bedroom where Angie stood.

"Turn around. Bend over and spread your cheeks!" Officer Dailey said.

"I'm not doing that," Angie said.

"Do it or I will charge you with resisting," Dailey said. "You could have already cheeked something by now."

"Gene Dailey?" I asked. "What are you doing?" Angie turned around and bent over.

"Are you getting an eye full?" she asked. Dailey smiled then looked for me to join in. "Stop doing that." I said to Angie. "Put something on."

"Hell no. Make sure I'm not carrying anything up my ass," she replied. "Would you like to stick your finger in there to make sure?"

"No, I would not!" I replied abruptly. "I ain't the one who made you do that. Stand up and put some clothes on. Now!"

"I was talking to Double-O-Dick-Dailey, not you." Angie said.

Dailey left the room smiling and began to search all the kitchen cabinets. He bragged the whole time to the chief about his encounter with Angie. I handed Angie a housecoat, and then said, "I had nothing to do with that."

"I know. It's Dailey," Angie said. "I can't stand him."

After the house was cleared, I walked outside to leave and was just behind Dailey. "I thought you said his house was full of dope," I asked.

"Training exercise!" Officer Dailey replied. "That skunk was sexy as hell though, wasn't she?"

"You're a strange man," I said, shaking my head.

●

In my opinion, that was Dailey's way of jamming the dagger just a little deeper into Kevin's back.

●

Not long after the search warrant was executed, Dailey took his family swimming at a pond just before the railroad tracks off Fifty Lakes Drive. Dailey ran into Kevin and Angie. "That's one of those cops," Angie told Kevin.

Dailey had to call Lieutenant Ledbetter and myself to bail him out of nearly getting his ass beaten by Kevin. I could see the fear in Dailey's eyes when I pulled up. "Serves you right," I said.

The Lieutenant made Kevin leave, even though he and Angie and Darren, had been at the pond first. My heart broke for Darren as Kevin carried him from the water. In my eyes, Dailey should've been the one to leave because Kevin was there first. I felt that Ledbetter's judgment made the entire force look bad.

CHAPTER 14

MIKE RAMOS

By the end of September 2006, I telephoned Adrian to get caught up on what he had done so far.

"I've hired a private investigator," he said.

"That's all?" I asked.

"To be court appointed, I've already done more than I normally would, and that's only because it's you."

I froze, totally stunned at what I had just heard. I had been taught in the police academy that the defendant was constitutionally entitled to the same legal representation by both *court appointed* and *retained attorneys,* so I didn't know how to respond to that. After we hung up, I hired Mike Ramos and then later told Adrian that he'd been fired. It would be years later before I discovered truly what Adrian meant by "to be court appointed."

Within a few months after we hired Mike Ramos, he became hard to deal with. He would never return my calls, emails, or letters.

By January 2007, after already paying him $15,000 dollars, he suddenly filed a motion to remove himself as counsel from my case. The reason he gave the court was that I failed to remit payment as agreed, which was true, but it still seemed odd.

I'll explain. Mike charged me $20,000 dollars with the agreement that I would send payment in increments of $5000 dollars over several weeks. My family and I were poor, very poor, but we banded together and, somehow, we all came up with the money. We had already made the first three payments on time, and I was having trouble coming up with the final $5000 dollars. At the last minute, a family member from out-of-state sold some property. I was only *one* week late with the final payment. Mike was not only previously notified of the problem, but he was also notified that the payment was on its way. So you can see why we were so concerned that he just up and filed a motion to remove himself.

Judge Ola Lewis denied his motion and told him, "Deal with it."

The damage was done though. Mike had quickly destroyed our relationship, so I became suspicious of his every move.

By March 2007, my case had gone through four prosecutors; Tiffany Campbell; Chris Jentry; some other new guy; and then finally, after nearly six weeks without any prosecutor, Meredith Everhart picked it up.

On April 7, 2007, I met with Mike Ramos, in a client-attorney conference room in the Brunswick County Courthouse. He called me the night before and said, "I must see you tomorrow morning. We have something to discuss."

I met Mike in the lobby, and when he first spotted me, he shook his head like he was disgusted about something. "Come on," he said. I followed him into a small conference room where he and I sat across the table from each other.

"Meredith said that she found pornographic pictures of Brittany on your home computer." Mike said.

My jaw hit the floor. "That's not true!" I protested

Mike thumbed through a folder and retrieved a photo. He held it up for me to see and asked, "Is this your computer?"

"Yes," I replied. "Actually, that's my son's computer, but they still didn't find any pictures like that."

"Was there another computer seized from your home?"

"No, but they still didn't find pictures of her from me," I replied. "We didn't have Internet at home yet, so how was I supposed to put the pictures on my computer?"

"I don't know. You tell me," he said. "I'm just telling you what Ms. Everhart said" Mike gave me the folder of Brittany's altered images. "I had them cover her body," he said. "Is that not Brittany?"

"Yes," I replied "But these pictures didn't come from my computer."

"You take the folder home and think about it," Mike said. "Call me later." He got up to leave, but I interrupted his escape.

"Did Brittany accuse me of having pictures of her?" I asked. Mike's response should've told me that something was brewing.

"She didn't have to," he said, and then he walked out of the room.

Danette and I sat at the kitchen table inspecting each picture carefully. The folder bulged with edited pornographic images of Brittany doing things with herself with some weird objects.

"She's one sick little girl." Danette said.

Several vulgar instant messages between Buddy and Brittany were mixed in the bunch, too. I got up to pour us both a fresh cup of coffee. Danette took the usual five teaspoons of creamer and sugar; mine doubled that amount.

"How am I gonna prove these pictures didn't come from me," I asked.

"I don't understand why they're trying to pin this on you," she said. "Whom have you pissed off? And why would Mike send you home with these pictures?"

I paused several seconds, recalling my conversation with Mike, and then it suddenly hit me. "Oh shit!" I said. "You don't think he's trying to...." I paused again, thinking of all the possibilities, and then I said, "What if someone's coming to do another search?" I asked. "How would I explain the pictures?"

"Surely to God, Mike wouldn't do that," Danette said. "You're just being paranoid."

I was paranoid. I was afraid that, any moment, someone would be knocking at the front door. *They'll never believe me.* I worried.

The next morning, I hid the folder under the spare tire in my trunk. I drove the 20 miles to Mike's office and I was trembling the entire trip. I couldn't help thinking, *Wouldn't this just be great if I got pulled over.*

I arrived at Mike's office at 8:30 a.m. and backed in next to the woods. I retrieved the folder from my trunk, opened it, and then looked through the pictures again. I searched for any trace, any hint, to prove the pictures didn't come from me.

Over the next twenty minutes, I looked up from the pictures, and scanned the cars as they passed, for any signs of Mike. I held up several pages of the forensic printouts and scanned each line carefully.

One of the reports reflected the following:

MAC Address: C40279PC

```
Workgroup: Workgroup
Computer Name: Home
        Operating System: Windows 98 Service Pack
        2
Type: jpeg Image
MS-DOS name: TOPLESS.JPEG
Created: July 26, 2006 10:22:00PM
Modified: July 26, 2006 10:22:00PM
Accessed: July 26, 2006 10:22:00PM
Location: D:/My Documents/Pictures
Drive Type: IDE
```

I examined the forensics repeatedly, carefully inspecting each page. Then, like a slap to the face, I had found it. Overwhelmed at my discovery, I called Danette. "You're never going to believe what I found!"

"What?" she asked.

"I'm on my way back home. I'll show you when I get there."

Once I returned home, I emailed Mike about the discovery. Days later, he still hadn't responded. I continued to leave numerous detailed messages at his office, but again, he never responded.

"Okay, mister." I said to myself, like I was talking to him, "We'll do this my way from here on out."

From that moment on, I wanted to fire Mike, but knew that it would be impossible to raise another $20,000 dollars or more. And don't think that I didn't try, but the thought of hitting my family up for another large sum of money bothered me immensely. We did find another attorney, but just couldn't come up with the additional $35,000 dollars.

PRIVATE INVESTIGATOR GENE HARDEE

Over the next year and a half or so, I barely spoke to Mike. On one of the few occasions when he contacted me on his own, he requested a meeting in his office on August 22, 2008 with a private investigator. I took my uncle, David Stidham, with me for my own protection, and to be my witness of anything that happened, or was said.

"This is Gene Hardee," Mike said, He will be the private investigator conducting some interviews for us."

"After all the test emails that we, Mister Mike Ramos, conducted, why did you wait until the last month to hire him?" I asked.

Mike didn't respond. Gene Hardee looked up, also waiting for a response, which surprised him, my uncle, and me.

"I am going to be busy for the next few days. Call Gene if you need me." Mike said.

"What good is that going to do?" I asked. "Are you going to call me back?"

Mike threw his jacket over his arm. "I've got to go to a meeting with the DA, I'm sorry." And with a slam of the door he was gone.

"Why did he wait so long to hire you?" I asked Gene.

"I don't know," he replied. "He didn't answer me either. I'll call you when I have something." Gene replied. I gave him my business number and address.

During that year and a half, while I was on house arrest, my brother and I had opened a garage on Village Road in Leland. It was called Brothers' Automotive. Within a few days of our meeting with Mike Ramos, Gene Hardee called me at the garage and set up a meeting. He and I sat in my office, going over my case, and I complained about Mike and how he had done nothing to prepare for my defense.

I suggested that Gene and I exchanged several emails, as Mike Ramos and I did, and then alter each other's contents at random. "Don't tell me what you're gonna change." I said. "Wait until I say go."

Later that evening, Gene emailed me a few times and I replied back to each one. "Let the games begin." I then wrote.

I changed every other word that he had typed, including the dates and time of the emails. Gene then replied, and altered what I changed. "I never knew that could be done." Gene wrote in his last reply. I had inserted all sorts of pictures and *almost* inappropriate content.

"See how easy it is to ruin someone's name?" I asked him.

At first, I was relieved to think that someone outside my family was listening. "I'll show this to Mike," Gene said.

●

As it turned out, even after Mike and I had done the same thing numerous times before, Gene would later see things Mike's way. I never heard from Gene after that email exchange until nearly *two years* later.

While in prison, I had my wife, Danette contact Gene Hardee to request that he mail me the test emails. Gene quickly refused. "But Luke needs it for his appeal," Danette explained on the telephone.

When Danette reminded him that he was paid to be *my* investigator, he told her to contact his attorney—Mike Ramos. Gene told Danette that he couldn't discuss any details and then told her he had nothing else to say.

I wrote Gene a letter from prison and conveyed to him that he couldn't use the same attorney as I was using due to reasons of conflict of interest. Gene went out and hired a second attorney, at the recommendation of Mike Ramos, of course.

Gene Hardee's new attorney mailed a letter to me, demanding that I desist from contacting Gene. "My client is not a party in your case," his new attorney explained. "You will need to contact Mike Ramos for the information you seek."

I wrote Mike to request Gene's report. He never responded. To this day, Gene's investigative reports and the test emails have never surfaced. I looked at it like this, if Gene Hardee had nothing to hide, why did he need to hire any attorney?

Why was he protecting Mike?

Why not just give me what I was entitled to?

Where are the test emails he and I conducted?

The answers became much clearer the further I kept going along.

CHAPTER 15

UNSPOKEN FORENSICS

It was Sunday morning, September 21, 2008, the day before my trial, when Mike called for a meeting. Having lost all trust in him, I took Danette, and Uncle David with me to be witnesses.

The conference room was actually Mike's office with a small computer in the corner. The back wall was shelved with legal books and binder folders. Mike's desk was a large conference table with stacks of papers lying all about. Mike and I sat across the table from each other. Danette and David sat behind me.

"Why haven't you or the State examined my two computers against hers?" I asked.

"They were not able to match up any email." Mike replied.

"You knew this all this time and didn't tell me?" I asked stunned at what I just heard.

"I mean they were not able to…. the emails were… They were not able to retrieve any emails," Mike stuttered. He sounded surprised, like he had just let the cat out of the bag.

"What," I replied and then slammed my fist on the table. I then lunged to my feet and confronted him, "You gotta be kidding me!"

I felt so much rage and betrayal because those emails, that I had denied writing all this time, were used as probable cause to secure my warrants. I paced the floor.

My imagination went wild as I thought about the extent of Mike's trickery, and that it had no boundaries.

"That's it. I'm not saying anything else," Mike said.

"You mean to tell me, you knew that the State didn't find any emails on his computers, and you never felt the need to tell us?" David asked.

"Why are you letting this happen?" Danette then asked, as she began to cry.

"Why have you not had full forensics conducted on my computers?" I asked. "Whose side are you on?"

Mike gave no response. He found it hard to look any of us in the eyes very long. Towered by two angry men, Mike squirmed around in his seat.

"Answer me!" I shouted, and for the second time, slammed my fist down.

"What is the most damaging evidence the State has?" David asked, as he placed his hand on my shoulder.

"The emails." Mike replied.

"Then why have you not…" I paused for a moment thinking, *You're not even going to try to defend me,* and then said, "You're going to get up there tomorrow and defend me against the emails. You're going to tell the judge that I didn't write those emails. You're going to show the test emails we conducted."

Mike responded by shaking his head, and then he said "I can't defend you against the emails."

"You're not even going to try?" Danette asked sobbing hard.

As her protector, the sight of my wife's hurt only infuriated me more. My jaws bulged as I bit down in anger.

"I'm starting to think you have mental problems," Mike said to me.

And that was all it took. I was pushed way beyond my limits.

"What did you say?" I asked, looking to fight. "What kind of deal did you make, huh?" I flung the few papers lying in front of me off the table. I'm normally not a violent man, but my body trembled in anger. The once mild-mannered gentlemen I hoped I had become, had turned into a nearly uncontrollable beast. "I have demanded that you file a change of venue. I will not get a fair trial here," I said

"Why have you ignored me?" I then asked, as my voice escalated until it strained.

"That's bullshit." Mike replied shouting. "You don't get one just because you want one."

"If we find out that you're letting him take the fall for something—you're going to have a bad day." David said.

"What are you going to do about...?" I started to ask, but then Mike interrupted, "I told you I got nothing else to say."

"So you're saying that you're not going to defend me then?" I asked.

Mike responded by shaking his head. He said, "I'm not going to lie for you."

"Lie for me?" I challenged. And that was about the end of that "meeting."

I stormed out of the office and Danette and David followed behind me. "That son-of-a-bitch thinks I wrote the emails." I said. "He's not even going to try to defend me."

On the drive home, very few words were spoken. "Are you okay, baby?" Danette asked.

"Just get me home," I responded.

No matter the outcome of the next day's trial, I knew it wouldn't be good. *I can't leave like this.* I reasoned to myself. If I were going to prison, I didn't want my last night with my wife and son to be a regretful memory.

After we returned home, I was eager to spend the last day of freedom in full swing. Over the past two years, I had discovered how to remove the house arrest bracelet. I had set up a low wattage lamp that mimicked my body heat.

I tricked the house arrest case managers into believing the ankle bracelet was too tight. I do have sort of large legs muscles so I used this as an excuse. I filed my heel down a little and slid the bracelet passed my ankle. I then placed it around the bulb.

It worked perfectly. I could be miles away and the electronic monitoring station never knew any different.

Danette and I drove to Wilmington that evening. We walked around the mall, never speaking of the earlier incident. I bought two candles from an aisle vendor. We later enjoyed a dimly lit dinner on the patio at Hara's Grill. We moved our evening to the beach and we were holding hands, trying to enjoy the last moments together.

A blanket of clouds hid the moon. Danette laid down a black sheet over the sand. The darkness hid our naked bodies, and for the next few hours, all worries, and any last memory of that day had faded away.

CHAPTER 16

TRIAL DAY

September 22, 2008. 8:30 am

Danette grabbed my hand, and we began to walk the 100-yard journey to the courthouse. Mike Ramos walked up just ahead. "Mike." I shouted.

He turned to look back and spotting my wife and me, he quickly hurried away.

"Something's wrong." I said.

A reporter from the *Star News* newspaper stood at the courthouse, waiting for us. Mike passed her and held out his hand as though blocking her from asking any questions. As my wife and I approached, she held up her camera.

"No pictures. No questions. No comments," I said, holding the door for Danette.

The reporter stalled a moment before she lowered her camera.

"I said no pictures!" I clearly and firmly reminded her.

Mike Ramos rushed into the elevator just before the doors closed.

My family and I waited just outside the courtroom "They can come get me when they're ready," I said. "Mike knows I'm here."

By now, the media had shown my face so much that every other person in the lobby stared at me. A man walked up to me with his hand extended and asked, "Do you remember me?"

"Not right off," I replied. He proceeded to tell me that he was the father of the two children he and I pulled on a raft through the floodwaters during Hurricane Irene. "I'm Larry. You carried my son on your back," he said.

Hurricane Irene flooded several streets in BSL, blocking exit routes from many of the neighborhoods. Larry's street was under four feet of water, and it began to overspill inside his mobile home. I was on duty that day and spotted Larry standing on the handrail flagging me down.

There was no way to drive to him, so I locked my radio and sidearm in the trunk, and then waded through the water. At one point, the water had risen almost to my chest.

"You have a good husband," Larry told my wife, adding to me, "By the way, I don't believe what they say. You don't strike me as that type of guy." Then he said, "Good luck, Officer Stidham."

I believe Larry sensed that my emotions were about to surface because he raised a hand to my shoulder. "You're a hero in my book," he said, which only made it harder for me to keep control. I could only nod my head a few times. He smiled and walked away.

8:45 am

Mike walked out from the courtroom. "The offer on the table is seventy-four months. Do you want it?" Mike asked.

"Hell no." I replied

"Do you want to replace me as your attorney?" Mike then asked shaking his head suggesting that I agree.

"Will the judge give me enough time to hire a new one?" I asked.

"He has to," he replied.

"You're fired then. Make it happen."

A look of relief came over Mike. He briefly smiled and then walked back into the courtroom. For a brief moment, I felt some relief, but that didn't last long and would only verify my skepticism even more.

11:00 am

Mike stepped just outside the courtroom doors "We're ready to start," he said.

●

The old courtroom was a three level building dominated by four large beige columns under the portico. Just beyond the metal detectors was a lobby with a half-mooned shaped staircase off to the left side leading to the second floor. Its balcony overlooked the first floor lobby.

The first floor consisted mainly of the District, Civil, and Juvenile Courtrooms. With all the Superior Courtrooms on the second floor, the third floor housed the District Attorney's offices, accessible by an elevator.

The courtroom was small, with either side only having 4-foot long church pews. The judge's bench was like a royal throne. It sat high on a raised dais. It was a dark stained mahogany frame overlaid with handcrafted trim of intricately carved vines and berries. The light fixtures were the normal two-by-two flush mounted fluorescents. The light arrangement above the judge's throne illuminated the judge as if he were the god of justice.

●

The courtroom quickly filled with my family members. Brittany had only her mother, Sherri, her mother's boyfriend, Lou Frankenburger, her dad, Johnny, and his girlfriend, Donna Millowsky.

Danette sat behind me shaking with fear. I had been her way of life for the last 15 years. I was all she knew.

I took my seat beside my incompetent attorney, but Mike turned away and faced the prosecutor. What small talk there was from among the courtroom officers soon turned to silence as the on-lookers gazed in awe.

The atmosphere in the courtroom was as thick as axle grease. Looking back at Danette, I camouflaged my enormous fear with another smile. In my heart, I knew the outcome of this trial had been predetermined as so many others were before me. I feared more for my wife and son than for myself.

"Madame Court Reporter and Madame Clerk, this is in the matter of Luther Luke D. Stidham. Mr. Ramos is his attorney and it's the first case for trial.

Your honor, Mr. Ramos indicated that Mr. Stidham was moving to have him relieved as counsel," Prosecutor Meredith Everhart said.

"All right. Mr. Ramos, do I hear from you, or do I hear from Mr. Stidham?" asked Judge Gary Locklear.

Judge Gary Locklear was a physically fit, short man with the ego of a king. He was called in as the emergency presiding judge because I had requested for Mike Ramos to move that Judge Ola Lewis recuse herself from my trial for several reasons.

At the time, I had only explained to Mike that I *knew* Ola and that it was in my best interest for her to recuse herself. But looking back now, I wished that I had told him the *real* reason.

Judge Lewis had agreed to the request and stated, "I don't want to hear his case anyway." She then quickly recused herself voluntarily, saving herself any further embarrassment or exposure through an actual motion in court.

Mike stated, "Your honor, I would just relate to you what I related in chambers. Mr. Stidham seems to be dissatisfied with my efforts and would ask to replace me."

Judge Locklear ordered, "Mr. Stidham, stand up. I want you to understand where we are in the process, as if you don't know; I know you do. Today is your trial date," Judge Locklear said. "Do you understand that?"

"Yes sir, I do."

"All righty then, tell me what is on your mind."

"Well, to begin with, I've requested four different times for a change of venue. I was ignored. Also, yesterday, I found out that there is possible evidence that hasn't been examined that could very well show my innocence." I continued, "In my eyes, there is evidence attempting to be presented that's come off one computer, and there's no other computer to compare it with. If they aren't willing to pull any files from my computer, I basically have no defense."

"Madame DA," Judge Locklear said, "Do you want to be heard?"

"Your honor, I'd say this case has been pending for two years. There has been ample opportunity to obtain *any* kind of experts that they wish." She went on to say, "There are two computers that were seized; one from the department's patrol vehicle and one from the police department at Boiling Spring Lakes.

"No full forensics was actually *requested* or *done* on the ones from the police department, and there has been two years to do that but no full forensics has ever been *requested* or *done*," the DA said. Then she continued, "Both Mr. Ramos and I are very prepared to go forward. He has done a *fine* job. I know from speaking with him, he's very ready and prepared to try this case. I see no reason to continue it at this point, or to release Mr. Ramos. I ask that you not release him, and keep the matter on the calendar for this week."

"Final comment, sir." Judge Locklear said crossing his arms a second time, and looking at me.

I stated, "There is forensic software that can be used to retrieve files to compare it, computer to computer, because I am disputing these emails. As of right now, Mike is telling me that they were unable to retrieve emails from my computers. The prosecutor is saying no forensics was *requested* or *done*. Something's not right." I said.

"Mr. Stidham? There's a jury coming, and you are telling me that you don't want Mr. Ramos to represent you. That puts you in a very awkward position. You are charged with two B-1 felonies, in addition to some much lesser matters," Judge Locklear stated to me. He added, "Unless there be any questions, let me remind you that for a level one, with *no* prior record, such as yourself, if you are convicted of a B-1 felony and there are two of them; it's a minimum of 16 years for just one. Madame DA has told me that she has made an offer and your attorney tells me he has communicated that offer to you," Judge Locklear said.

"Yes, sir."

"I want you to understand this," Judge Locklear added, "if this matter goes to a jury—and at some point it *will*, with Mr. Ramos, or without him, it's going to go to trial. And I don't know that the facts are going to change by a delay in these proceedings. I can't imagine that this case would stand or fall on the production of emails. This is a factual issue. Did you or did you not do the things that you were accused of. Not did you or did you not use a computer."

But how can I prove I didn't commit the act if I'm not allowed to dispute the evidence? I wondered, as the judge went on.

"That's not one of the elements, emailing somebody. The bottom line is this: my inclination is to not allow Mr. Ramos out of this case, period. But if you insist on relieving Mr. Ramos, that leaves you in the posture of representing *yourself*, because there is going to be a jury here in an hour and a half—two hours.

"Again, there's too much at stake to find yourself representing yourself. However, I cannot compel you to be represented in any way by Mr. Ramos. If you tell me that you don't want him to be your lawyer, *do you understand?*" Judge Locklear asked, and then he paused before continuing, "I am not going to grant a continuance in this case. That leaves you representing yourself. Do ... you ...

understand?" Judge Locklear said a second time and in a fashion that told me to read between the lines.

I paused several seconds before I replied, "Yes I do."

"Well then, Mr. Ramos is in this case until you tell me he's not.... Yes, sir?" Judge Locklear asked, as I raised my hand.

"May I make one more statement?" The judge nodded his head and then dropped it into his hands.

"Computers will copy the code embedded in emails. So, may I ask for a continuance long enough to have my computers examined?" I said. Then I continued, "You see, when emails are deleted, it's the server that they're deleted from, not the user's computer. The code will still be there, and *can be* retrieved by forensic science. They can be."

"I understand the dilemma that you find yourself in," Judge Locklear said. "However, the bottom line is this, if the State felt it necessary to get this information from that source, I assume they would have sought out that information."

●

I had no idea at the time that Meredith Everhart; AKA "the State," had already sought out that information, and I guess when considering what she and Ghent had found, it was in both Brittany's and the State's best interest to keep it a secret. And that they did... Until now.

●

"I understand you claim you need it. I'm sorry. I stand by my ruling, and that is Mr. Ramos is in the case until you tell me he's not. It's that simple," Judge Locklear said. "Are there other matters that need to be heard in this matter?" he then asked Meredith.

"Yes, sir," she replied.

"We need to let these parties stand down and have a discussion, to the extent that they *can* or *will*, and then come back and re-visit. I hope to hear a report from one or both of you in 30 minutes." Judge Locklear said.

CHAPTER 17

INNOCENT MEN GO TO PRISON EVERY DAY

I didn't wait for the judge to dismiss us; I got up and walked out. My family was quick to join me.

"Mr. Stidham, I need to see you." Mike said, trying to catch up to us.

"You can go to hell, Mike." I said, feeling like a cornered rat.

I walked to the edge of the second-story ledge and leaned on the handrail. Danette walked up behind me and rubbed my back, saying. "I'm sorry baby. They're not going to give you a chance."

"Why?" I asked. "What the hell have I done to deserve this?"

My uncle David walked up and stood beside me, offering his view, "The judge is acting as if he is completely ignorant of the emails. I don't understand." He then added, "It's like they are trying to avoid a forensics at all cost."

"This whole case has already been decided," I replied. I knew then, without a doubt, my case had already been decided. I had to say it out loud, "I don't stand a chance."

Mike approached us, careful not to walk up too fast. He said, "We have to talk."

I turned around and asked him, point blank, "Why didn't you tell the judge about all our test emails?"

Not waiting for Mike's answer, Danette interrupted, "He was with me and two other people. How can you let an innocent man go to prison?" She was scared, shaking, and letting her tears fall, as she held tight to my arm.

"Innocent men go to prison every day!" Mike Ramos snapped at us. He turned to me, "What are you going to do, Luke?"

I felt the anger surge up from the floor. It climbed through my legs until it exploded in my head. I had no idea what else to do. I'd lost all last remaining shreds of doubt that Mike had truly joined the prosecution. He wanted a conviction just as badly as Meredith Everhart did.

"Do you accept the plea, or not?" Mike asked

"No I don't!" I shouted. Mike turned and walked back into the courtroom.

I wanted to fight Mike so badly that I probably would have nearly beaten him to death, given half a chance.

"I know you don't want to hear this, but Mike is not going to defend you. You will lose, and then you're looking at forty years in prison," David said. "Five years is a whole lot better than forty."

David was right, and I knew it. I still didn't want to face the fact. To take the plea would be I would be admitting I was guilty. And I wasn't!

"Baby, maybe you should take the plea," Danette added.

I felt overwhelmed with fear, disappointment, and so much confusion. I felt hopeless. I had to think and think quickly. "On one hand, if I don't take the plea, I'll go to prison for the rest of my life. On the other hand, I'll go to prison for five years, AND I'll be branded as a sex offender forever" I said.

Mike walked from the courtroom with a folder in his hand. He told me the judge had offered to lower my plea offer down to a 54-month minimum *if* I would take the plea.

"I don't have much of a choice, do I?" I asked Mike. "The judge isn't going to allow me any defense and you… You knew all about it, didn't you?"

"There's no time for this," Mike said. "There's only a small window. Ms. Everhart objects, but the judge has overridden her."

"What about the two-years house arrest?" I asked. "Don't I get credit for that?"

"If that is what you have to have, but you have to decide now." Mike replied.

"Get all my credit. I'm not moving until then." I said.

"Luke, if you don't take this plea, you will be an old man when you get out of prison." Mike said. "I cannot defend you against the emails. Take the damn plea."

I felt like I had no more choices. My mind was spinning, searching for reason, but at the same time my mind was just played out and empty as a dry well. I was lost in utter fear.

Mike examined my expression and then quickly disappeared inside behind the courtroom doors. I think that is when Danette finally realized, too, that I was doomed. "They're not giving you any choice in this matter." She cried. "I don't know what else to do."

Danette was traumatized by my soul-wrenching experience. My heart broke for her because I knew that she would soon be on her own, and I could do nothing to stop it. I could do nothing to help her, support her, or to reassure her. She had grown to look to me as her provider, and I felt that I had failed her.

Moments later, Mike exited the courtroom doors. "Luke? I got your credit but we have to act now."

"If I go to trial and lose, can I appeal?" I asked.

"You stand little to no chance at an appeal," Mike replied. "Are you backing out now?"

"No, but you're rushing me," I replied. "If I take the plea, it's an Alford plea with my credit." I added.

An Alford plea was simply a plea of neither guilt nor non-guilt, but an acceptance that there was enough evidence to warrant a conviction. At the time, it at least felt comforting that I could salvage what was left of my life without a plea of guilt.

"I'll be back in a minute for you to sign the papers." Mike said, as he rushed off to the elevator.

"One more thing," I insisted. Mike stopped and turned around. I looked him in the eye and said, "I turn myself in tomorrow, not today. I want to tell my son good-bye. That's the deal or nothing." Then tears began to run down my face.

Thirty minutes later, Mike stepped out from the elevator with a handful of papers. A sign of accomplishment was spread across his face.

"Mr. Stidham? I need you to come with me," he said. *So now I'm Mr. Stidham.* I wondered.

I followed Mike into a small conference room. "I ain't doing this alone." I said, and then stepped back out to call for my uncle. We entered a conference room and David and I sat down across the table, both of us facing Mike.

He said, "You're giving up your attorney-client privilege by having him present."

"What privilege?" I asked, sarcasm dripping from each word. "He's my witness."

Mike said, gathering the papers in a neat stack. "This is real simple. Just sign the plea. I got the judge to agree to you coming in tomorrow."

He turned the documents around and slid them a few inches toward me. I began reading through the plea agreement and all the other documents.

"Wait. Where's my house arrest credit?" I asked, but then found something else that was far worse and far more disturbing. "What is this second degree rape about?" I asked. "I wasn't accused of rape."

"I'll be requesting the credit in court." Mike replied.

"Does that mean that I'll get it?"

"Yes. It's part of the deal."

"The rape's not," I said. "I ain't signing this."

Mike said, "I made a mistake on the original offer. Also, once we begin the proceeding, you won't be allowed to speak anymore. If you have any other concerns ask me now."

"I don't care what kinda mistake you made." I responded.

"Whose side are you on?" David interrupted, glaring at Mike.

Mike never took his eyes off of me, nor did he answer David's question. He insisted,

"You're going to have to finish up; they're waiting on us. If you don't sign the plea, you know what the alternative is."

"I'm not signing the rape," I said. "It is what it is."

"It's your funeral," Mike replied.

CHAPTER 18

11:45 PM

Brittany, surrounded by Agent Ghent and her family, wept carelessly on cue and loudly as I passed her in the aisle. I took my seat just as the prosecutor began to speak.

"We are back on the record in the matter of Luther Luke Stidham. He's charged with two counts of indecent liberties with a minor, and by way of Bill of Information, one count of second degree rape," DA Everhart said. "Mr. Ramos? How does your client plead?"

"Your honor, he tenders a plea of guilty pursuant to North Carolina vs. Alford." Mike replied.

"If I may approach with a plea transcript and the worksheet?" Everhart asked.

"Please, and there is the Bill of Information which requires your client's signature," Judge Locklear replied, as he looked to Mike. Mike responded by nodding his head.

I stared straight ahead. I kept my eyes fixed on a light switch mounted on the wall across from me. I shook my head and tapped my fingers on the table in disbelief. I fought the urge to shout, *"Stop! Stop! Take me to trial."* When I heard the judge speak about the second-degree rape, I leaned to Mike. "I ain't signing shit. Don't even ask."

"You don't have a choice." Mike replied.

I had been beaten.

It was over.

All I could do was cross my arms and continue to stare at the wall. David leaned forward in his seat to observe Brittany's actions.

He told me later that Brittany was crying uncontrollably and for real then. Sherri Lewis, her mother, was trying to hug her, but Brittany kept pushing her off. Brittany spoke quietly to her mother and David said he thought he read Brittany's lips fairly well and told me he thought Brittany said, "This ain't supposed to happen,"

Johnny Lewis, seeing that Brittany was causing attention to be drawn to them, moved to sit beside her, telling her, "What are you trying to do?" Stop and sit still!" He gripped Brittany's leg in an attempt to stop it from shaking. She covered her eyes with several pieces of tissue papers.

"And, Your Honor, as soon as the plea's done. I'll be providing the clerk with dismissals for the statutory sex offense and statutory rape charges," Everhart said.

"All right, the judge said, then he added, "If you'd stand, Mr. Stidham, you'll find a Bible there in front of you, sir. Place your left hand on the Bible, raise your right hand, and take this oath." Judge Locklear turned and said, "Madame Clerk?"

MANUFACTURED FACTUAL BASIS

After the clerk administered the oath, I sat down, forced to listen – and forced to make my family listen -- to the most bizarre story about how the alleged consensual sexual intercourse accusation against me suddenly changed to "ravish," and "by force," and "against Brittany's will."

DA Everhart began, "If this matter had gone to trial, the state's evidence would show that on or around the eleventh day of September, 2006, Detective Simpson of the Brunswick County Sheriff's Department, was notified by Lou Frankenburger, and Mrs. Sherri Lewis, of possible sexual encounters between the defendant and their daughter, Brittany Lewis. Detective Simpson contacted the State Bureau of Investigation because the defendant was an active police officer with the Boiling Spring Lakes Police Department and requested their assistance.

"The victim in this case had recently been released from care at the Brynn Marr Hospital following a suicide attempt by taking too many Tylenol pills on the thirty-first day of August 2006. After she was released, she told her mother and stepfather that a large part of why she had taken the pills was because she and the defendant had sexual contact.

"Detective Simpson interviewed Brittany, and she informed her that they had met during the month of July 2006, and that initially she had gone on a ride-along with him in his police car. That ride was approved by her father, and an official ride-along form was filled out and that type of thing.

"After she went on this first sanctioned ride-along, the evidence would show at some point the defendant suggested through email, that she actually sneak out of her house, *against* her father's will—wishes, after he was asleep and meet him for additional ride-along. She and two of her friends, Jee Holton and Clara Millings snuck out of her house after midnight on two occasions when the defendant was on duty. That he came and met them in his patrol SUV, picked them up and took them on a ride-along, and Brittany will testify that on those two unsanctioned ride-along, that she kissed the defendant or that they engaged in kissing between the two of them and that would be the basis for the two indecent liberties with a minor charges.

"The final charge of second-degree rape occurred on morning of the twenty-third day of August 2006, when they had discussed meeting at two o'clock in the morning at a similar place that they had previously met.

"The evidence would show that, that night they did, in fact, have sex in his patrol vehicle. That there was both vaginal and digital penetration, but the force alluded to in the second-degree rape charge was that the defendant was abusing his position, power, and discretion as a police officer.

"Brittany had told Officer Stidham on multiple occasions that she had thought of ending her life and that she had contemplated suicide. The defendant took advantage of her emotional state.

"Brittany informed the detective that after she had sex that night that essentially the defendant had cut off all ties with her and at that point, she decided to attempt to take her life." Everhart concluded.

Judge Locklear asked, "Regarding the factual basis, Mr. Ramos, any additions or deletions?"

"No, sir," Mike said.

UNSIGNED BILL

After the judge sentenced me 54 months behind bars, Mike took me to a small client room where he tried again to force me to sign the Bill of Information. I refused. He threatened that all deals were off and said, "If you don't, you won't see home again for a long time."

I snatched up his pen and then *wisely* signed near the middle of the page, leaving the defendant's signature box empty.

Mike freaked, "That's not going to work." He grabbed the Bill of Information and told me to stay put.

I waited about two minutes after he left and then got the hell out of Dodge. I ran out of the client room, grabbed my wife's hand, and hurried her down the staircase and through the front doors. On the drive home, I explained to her what had happened. She called the family, who were all still back at the courthouse and had no idea what had just happened. Once we got home, I kept waiting for someone to knock at our door, but no one did, so I made the best of what I had left.

CHAPTER 19

MY LAST NIGHT

That's a day that I will never forget. I was angry at the whole world. I had so much hatred in me. Brittany had just sat in her seat, leaning forward and crying the whole time I was forced to answer yes to all the Court's questions about the plea. Brittany's sobbing got even worse after she covered her face in grief when the judge sentenced me to 54 months behind bars. She knew she had messed up. I think she had just let it go too far and she didn't know how to stop it, or better yet, I think I've now figured out—someone wouldn't let her, and for their own good reasons, too.

Later that evening, my uncle David decided to treat everyone to dinner. It was going to be my last steak dinner for a while. My nerves were so torn-up that it was all I could do to eat anything. And I'm a steak-lover too.

My last night with my wife and family was not an easy one. I don't remember sleeping, only lying in bed trying to act like I was okay. I prayed that night that God would just take me.

We all woke up around seven o'clock the next morning. I knew that everyone couldn't help but wonder how I felt.

I felt like I was in the spot light. Imagine knowing that you must turn yourself over to a handful of corrupt judicial conspirators for the next four-and-a-half years, knowing that you are completely innocent, and there's nothing you can do about it? At least, not yet, anyway.

There wasn't much conversation that morning. Everyone just kept hugging on me and crying. After breakfast, we took a bunch of pictures together, and then got ready to leave.

I handed Danette my driver's license, wedding ring (for fear of losing it in prison), and my watch. I gave Nathan my old badge and police ID. "Hold on to this until I return." I told them both. We loaded up and looked like a convoy driving down Hwy 87.

The closer we got, the more frightened I became. When we took that last turn into the jail's parking lot, I almost had a panic attack. I could hardly breathe.

We arrived just before 9 am. We had a little time to waste, so we just stood around the parking lot and savored the last few moments we had together.

At nine-thirty, everyone walked me in. I walked up to the window and said, "I'm Luther Stidham, I'm supposed to report to jail to start my prison sentence."

"No one has told me anything about it. It will be a while," a voice said through the intercom. "Just have a seat, sir."

"Have a seat my ass." I replied, and I walked right through the exit door.

Oh how I wanted to leave. What are they going to do? Withdraw the plea? I wondered.

The deputy called for me after about an hour. My family and I walked close to the last door that I would pass through separating me from freedom for many years to come.

A large gray security door opened, and a deputy stood waiting for me in the doorway. I said my good-byes one more time.

I saved the best for last, my wife. I savored every second of her. Danette wrapped her arms tightly around me and then laid her head on my chest. Her whole body shook. She and I gently swayed back and forth in our own little embrace.

"I love you, Luke." She whispered. Her undertone surrendered to a hard cry, as she said, "Please don't go."

I had to pull loose from her grip.

That day was so horrible. Their cries got louder, and as I inched closer to the door, my brother, father-in-law, and nephews started crying. Everyone was crying now, except me. I was still in shock I think, unsure of reality at that moment. It was like a bad dream and I didn't know if I wanted to wake up or not.

I walked backwards to the steel door behind me. I tried my best to put on a brave face. I felt the emotions about to overcome me so I turned away and took that last step. Tears then ran like rivers. I tried as hard as I could not to make any noise. I bit down hard on my bottom lip hoping to hold it together as my ribs quivered.

The metal door slammed closed behind me, and what happened next, buckled my knees.

"Oh God!" Danette screamed out. "No! No!" It sounded like she was in such horrendous pain. I completely lost it. I balled up my fists and nearly swung on the deputy standing in the corridor with me. He backed up, raised his hands, and then said, "I got nothing to do with this, Officer Stidham."

CHAPTER 20

PIEDMONT CORRECTIONAL INSTITUTE

The deputy locked me in a holding cell while I waiting to be transported to prison. After a couple of hours, another deputy, a tall, burly man, opened the door and said, "You're out of here." I guess, because of the corridor incident, they felt that I was a threat. Maybe I was.

He cuffed my hands and legs then attached a chain to my leg irons. My chain was so short I had to bend over a little. I could only take small, baby steps as I inched my way to the van.

Another prisoner going to be processed at Piedmont Correctional Institute joined me. "Aren't you that cop?" this guy asked after the van door was closed.

"Was." I responded.

"So how's it feel to be on this side for a change?" he asked.

"It feels like shit," I replied. I didn't feel much like talking so I leaned down and slept most of the ride from Bolivia to Salisbury.

When we arrived at PCI, "Oh shit," was the only thing I could get out. I think I almost hyperventilated, too. I could hardly catch my breath. Here I was, a former cop convicted of rape and taking indecent liberties with a child, now in prison—a deadly combination.

Honestly, I was also scared to death. If I'd been given just one chance, I would've run my ass off. Either they would have shot me, or I would have gotten away. Regardless, I would have accepted either fate at that moment. I felt like everyone knew who I was, so I watched everyone carefully.

●

PCI is a medium-custody camp, double-fenced, wrapped in rows of razor wire, and cornered by gun towers. It has a high-rise building where most of the assigned inmates were housed. Since PCI is also a processing camp, it has a separate fenced-in, single-story housing unit called J-208. All the recently sentenced inmates are temporarily housed in J-208, while they undergo medical treatment and evaluation. Once the inmate has completed his exams, he is assigned a camp, and then he just waits to be shipped, like a piece of freight.

●

As our van pulled up to the sally port, the door lifted, and we pulled inside. The door was an enormous, reinforced garage door. Although today it would probably sound like any other heavy-duty garage door, that day, it had a monstrous growl as it closed down behind me with a finality that sounded like doom. I cringed as I heard it and my knees went weak. The hairs on my arms and neck stood up. My whole body jerked.

"This is it," I said. "Here we go."

The back doors to the van opened, and I had to wait until my name was called to exit.

"Inmate Stidham!" The voice came from a large prison guard.

In prison, we were rarely called "Mister "anymore. It was mostly just "Inmate."

I exited the van and walked toward the large guard. He pointed to a double door. I nodded my head and thought the doors would automatically open. In doing so, I almost ran into them.

"Wait for the other guard to open the doors," said the large prison guard with an attitude that suggested that I should've known better.

Once inside, another guard took us one by one and searched us. "Take off all your clothes and lay 'em on the counter!" The guard barked. "Lift your stuff."

"Like I can really hide something under my Johnson," I thought.

"Turn around, bend over and spread 'em."

I was so humiliated as I stood there, naked. It felt like I was standing nude in front of a church congregation. It was a busy hallway, too. As I stood there bent over with my bunghole shining, both men and women walked by like it was nothing. The guard had latex gloves on, too, so I thought, *"I hope like hell you're not about to stick your finger up my ass."* Thankfully, he never violated me.

After he searched me, I was directed down the hallway to take a shower and then get dressed in my new uniform—medium custody brown canvas pants with a white T-shirt. I was then directed further down the hallway to have my picture taken. I was so sad that day. I wanted to find a hole to fall in and cover myself up. The guard said, "Say cheese," in a tone of sick, sour humor, but I just couldn't hide my emotions too well. I was fighting tears as I looked at the camera.

As I waited for my new prison ID card and cell assignment, I was ordered to sit on a bench covered in graffiti, dried spit, and blood. I wondered if I would survive for the next 54 months. I tried to imagine what it was going to be like, drawing all my perceptions from those lock-up TV shows. My thoughts and those images made it more difficult than it turned out to be, but I didn't have any way of knowing that on my first day. I shook in un-necessary fear.

After I was processed, I was taken to segregation. I had to be in protective custody the first two days because of my status as a cop.

Segregation is considered being in "the hole," and believe me, they can have it. I had a small window about 8 inches wide by 24 inches tall. As I looked out of the window, it appeared that I was on the top floor.

I guess it had not really sunk in until I unpacked what little belongings I had, issued by the prison, on a shelf under my stainless steel bed frame. My mattress was about two inches thick and lumpy, as was my pillow. I made my bed and sat down. I took in a long breath, and that's when it hit me. *"How in the hell am I going to survive another five years like this?"*

I truly wished for death then, thinking, *"Just kill me and get this over with."* I thought – and hoped – God would give just an ounce of mercy to me.

Looking around, I realized there was nothing I could use to cut my wrists. I thought about ramming my head into the corner of my bed frame, but hell, it would've taken more than just once, and besides that, it would hurt like hell. I wasn't up for too much more pain at that point. A quick slice of my wrist and it would be over; no more feeling betrayed by my own kind.

Disappointed that I had nothing to end this cruelty, I got up off the bunk and walked over to the window again. I could see a small housing development, woods, and a few streets—all the normal stuff that just less than twenty-four hours earlier I had seen through my own free eyes, and had taken for granted. I stared out that window for hours.

It was getting dark and the moon was bright. It lit up the prison yard pretty well. I could see every detail in the grass, from the footprints to the tire tracks. It was such a beautiful night. I tried to imagine what Danette was doing at that very moment.

"When am I gonna see you again?" I asked of nobody. I found myself feeling extremely depressed and suicidal again. Everything was all wrong. I kept telling myself that this would never last.

"Brittany will come forward or I'll appeal." I thought.

●

I think now, looking back, that's how I survived all that time, thinking I would get out. Hell, we all do, I guess. It keeps us, the "Inmates" sane to a point. For several years to come, I fought hard at my appeal. Little did I know that Judge Ola May Lewis would be waiting to devour me.

●

As quickly as I felt a moment of relief, depression set in again. I wondered why I was having such a hard time dealing with my incarceration.

"*Am I a sissy?*" I wondered.

Today, I believe it was the fact that I had been so wronged that got me through, day to day to day, all the while planning my counter attack. Had I been guilty, maybe I could have dealt with it better. But I wasn't, so being convicted for what I had not done was hard to fathom.

Hell, it still is.

I tried to sleep, hoping to forget where I was. When I woke, it was like a cruel joke getting played over and over.

At about three o'clock that next morning, after hours of staring at the night light in my cell, I seriously debated suicide or escape again.

"*How can I kill myself without killing myself?*" I wondered, as I thought about the "NO WARNING SHOTS" theory. *But I can't do that to my family,* I finally reasoned.

I sat up, pondered for a minute, and then decided to do what they never expected of me....

MODERN DAY SCARLET LETTER

As I look back on the years past, the lies, cover-ups, and conspiracy, all the events that led to my incarceration, played in my mind every day.

Politically, my trial hearing, all the pointless motions I had filed, and Judge Ola Lewis's interference in my appeal process could not have been uglier. It had taken its toll.

There were many days in prison when the depression had overwhelmed me. On those days, dark forces consumed me and the thoughts of suicide were frequent as I imagined what my future held.

Where would I live? Who would even hire me?

The questions were endless. I kept going back to the one thing that haunted me the most, the modern day "Scarlet Letter."

I'm damned for the rest of my time on earth. I'm better off dead, I concluded, and you'll soon learn why.

Had I been on a gun camp, the chance that I would have tested the "NO WARNING SHOT" theory again seemed more likely than not.

On days like those, I found strength in God, and inspiration from reading anything that I could get my hands on. I was a magazine man. I kept stacks of all the latest editions in my locker.

I preferred *Time, People, Rolling Stone, Newsweek, Reader's Digest, Publisher's Weekly,* and *GQ.* Their stories would capture my imagination to a point that I could drift away to a much better place. It wouldn't be long before I was completely emerged. This hostile environment would slowly fade, and then I stood on a beach in Hawaii or attended a film festival with Johnny Depp in Canada.

Everything that I've shared with you so far would be in vain if I didn't also admit that in some way, each magazine played its own part in saving my life.

NEARLY THERE

As I sit here in my own small corner of Gaston Correctional Center's B Dorm wrapping up the last few details of this book, I am just 89 days from freedom. Christmas is in four days, and this is the last one I'll spend alone.

It's been such a long and hard road now, and I want you know that I am eager to rejoin you in the free world, yet still frightened as hell of what's to come. I don't know what the future holds for me. With Judge Ola Lewis still in office and hot on my heels, I may never see a favorable outcome. So I wrote this book with several goals in mind.

Mainly, to demystify my guilty plea for the wonderful people of Boiling Spring Lakes, NC, my rookie class and instructors, Mr. Lindsey and Ms. Donna, and one of the officers at the Oak Island Police Department. I also wrote this book for the people I cared most about, besides my own family: Erica, Toots, Scott, Danielle, Ronnie, and the Warren family, just to name a few.

The substance of conversations during my trial hearing was taken directly from the court reporter's certified transcript and placed in this book. I eliminated redundant and irrelevant information but it closely matched the documentary record.

All the charges I faced were real, with two categorized as B1 felonies. The only charge higher was First Degree Murder - a class A felony. The bare minimum sentence for just one B1 was 114 months behind bars. Combined, I faced up to 40 years without the lesser offenses.

With a court-forced attorney, and stripped of all defense, I had given up all hope of a fair trial. I had no other logical choice; I had a family to think about. My choice was simple: five years or a minimum of 40? I wasn't going to win. Mike Ramos, Charles Ghent, and Meredith Everhart had already seen to that.

But I also wrote this book for me. I wanted to tell my story, what *really* happened, in my own words, and now I'm ready to just move on with my life.

And finally, to become the forum that gives the poor, the uninformed, as well as the underachievers, a voice, by exposing what it feels like when the law turns against you. It's important to know that I'm not alone; that other people were given the same coerced choices and forced to surrender one constitutional right in order to assert another.

My one wish is that you've gained the confidence to believe in me, and when the time comes, take a stand with me.

In closing, I'll share a bit of inspiration passed onto me by a wise man in prison.

Since my first arrival at Gaston Correctional Center in April 2009, I became the teacher's assistant in their Human Resources Development course. The class had left the room for their usual 10-minute break, and I stayed behind to speak with our guest speaker, Glenn Smith, a three-time author, and sociologist.

Glenn, who knew very little about my case, asked, "How far would you go to prove you're innocent?" I leaned back in my chair and pondered several minutes over the question.

Some three years later, my answer's the same today as it was back then,

"You're looking at it!"

Giving up just won't be an option because I am, eleven seventy-seven, falsely accused forever branded.

-Luther Stidham

EPILOGUE

It is *per se* ineffective for trial counsel to join the prosecution in an effort to secure a conviction by stripping a defendant of his only opportunity to put the state's evidence through rigorous testing.

This book deals with the question of whether it is acceptable for prosecutors and defense attorneys to both lie in court and to clients about their defense prospects to maintain their currency in court. The defendant has the constitutional right to present all matters of legal merit that are necessary to complete a competent defense.

Our courts should not encourage their bar members to do the court a favor by lying to clients and omitting issues to maintain their currency so they can succeed on other days, in other cases, and on other issues.

In this nation, rights, laws, and technicalities should apply to us all, and it should be the job of the attorney to go into court and make sure our judges are observing them, even if it means rubbing their faces in due process. Unfortunately, rather than upholding this bare necessity, our nation's courts encourage attorneys to be mindful of their social, political, and financial currency more so than any underlying issues, the merits of law, or the rights of the defendant.

Mike Ramos's deficiency prejudiced my case with respect to a necessity defense in a manner so serious as to deprive me of a fair trial and likely acquittal, and for what I ask? The answer is simple: To maintain his "currency" with the court and favor with Meredith Everhart so that he could succeed on other days, in other cases, and on other issues.

This ineffective assistance of counsel resulted not only from Mike's errors or misconduct, but also from restraints imposed by the trial court that rendered even the best ambitions of the most capable counsel ineffective, by allowing perfunctory pursuit of latitudes ripe for conviction while denying any pursuit of merits ripe for acquittal.

It is my goal, rather than upholding this ideal, to encourage attorneys to go to battle for the rights of the client. It's just what good attorneys do.

I don't want to be remembered as the cop accused of bumping ugliness with a 14-year-old girl. Besides, there's a saying among the *Thin Blue Line* community, "the badge will get a man all the 'vagina' he wants." And that was the clean version.

Honestly, I want to be remembered as one of the best storytellers around but if I'm doing my part to protect human rights and influence equality among all people, I feel good about what I'm doing. I feel like that can be my biggest contribution to society.

APPENDIX A:

ACTUAL CASE FILES AND REPORTS

Besides conforming to the name changes throughout this book, in some instances, the contents of the forthcoming actual case file documents were edited to eliminate redundant and irrelevant information. Again, these are the ACTUAL CASE FILES.

By the end of November 2008, I had begun my appeal process. My family and I wrote and called Mike Ramos countless times requesting the case file. I quickly became suspicious when Mike never responded, and by March 2009, had no other choice but to file a grievance against him with the NC State Bar.

After the lengthy grievance process, and countless more letters and telephone calls, Mike finally surrendered my file. Over all, it would take some 13 months after my conviction before I actually got my hands on my case file.

What I discovered next caused me to gasp in my seat. I was so upset that I became nauseated. My hands were shaking in anger from feeling betrayed, and I could hardly contain my fury. And then Mike added insult when he included this actual apology letter:

Ramos and Lewis, LLP
1010 Sellers Road
Shallotte, NC 28459
October 15, 2009

RE: contents of file

Dear Mr. Stidham:
Please be advised, the contents of your entire file, in my possession, has been sent to:

Davidson Stidham
23151 Johnstine Road
Charlotte, NC 28269

I apologize for the delay in getting the documents to you. It was my understanding that your wife was going to come by the office to pick them up.

Very truly yours,
Mike Ramos

As you can image, I wrote Mike back. "I never once told you that my wife would drive nearly 400 miles to pick up my case file. You're just trying to cover up for your negligence." I then pointed out three very important mistakes he had made in his letter.

"Otherwise, first, who gave you permission to mail evidence involving certain juvenile victims in a sex offense case to a non-party individual? Second, how else would you have known to send my case file to my uncle, and last, how did you get his address?"

After a few days, my uncle David reviewed the case and then he told me on the telephone that I wouldn't believe what Mike had held back from us.

David then mailed all the suppressed documents to me, and after I read through each one, I wrote Mike again. "You had all this evidence in your possession the whole time and you didn't tell me?" Mike never responded, and perhaps, what we discovered better explained why:

DETECTIVE SIMPSON'S INCIDENT REPORT

On September 11, 2006, Brunswick County Deputy Simpson met with Ms. Sherri Lewis and her boyfriend, Lou Frankenburger at the Brunswick County Sheriff's Office. Deputy Simpson's report reflected the following activity took place:

On 09/11/2006, Ms. Lewis came in to report that her 14-year-old daughter had just been released from Brynn Marr Hospital on 09-07-2006, and on the following day, Brittany Lewis disclosed that she had sexual contact with a Boiling Spring Lakes Police Officer.

Sherri explained that Brittany was sent to the hospital for about a week because she had tried to kill herself by taking an overdose of Tylenol. Sherri explained that her daughter, Brittany, had been living with her father, Johnny T. Lewis, in Boiling Spring Lakes when the overdose took place. Sherri explained that when Brittany was released from the hospital, she moved in with her on Danwood Road.

Lou explained that he had asked Brittany to tell him why she was spreading rumors that a fireman named, Buddy, raped her.

Lou explained that Brittany was very upset and crying and she then told him that she was not the one saying she was raped, that she did have sex with him, and that she had also had sex with a police officer named, Luke.

Lou explained that neither he nor Brittany's mother knew if Brittany was being truthful because she had been doing a lot of sneaking out, not being truthful with them and using her mother and father against each other.

Lou explained that on the night of Brittany's suicide attempt, Officer Stidham told them that Brittany had accused her father of molesting her.

Lou explained that Johnny told him that Officer Stidham also reported that Brittany had been stalking him, calling him all the time, and would show up during the night at the store or park when he was working.

Lou explained that he and Sherri waited until Brittany went to school today to talk to the police because they did not want to upset her. They do not want to make false allegations against a police officer if Brittany was making up lies.

I asked Sherri how long Brittany had been giving her and her father problems. Sherri stated for several months. Sherri stated that Brittany had been running away, cutting her wrist, and drinking alcohol.

09/11/2006: Approximately 11:30 a.m. I made contact with Chief Deputy Cotswald and he advised me to conduct an interview with Brittany.

09/11/2006: Approximately 2:30 p.m. I conducted an interview with Brittany Lewis. The interview was *video* and *audio* recorded.

After conducting the interview with Brittany, I debriefed Special Agent Charles L. Ghent from the North Carolina State Bureau of Investigation about the allegations, and at which time, Agent Ghent, was introduced to Brittany. Agent Ghent took over as the investigating officer.

AGENT GHENT'S AFFIDAVIT

Agent Ghent's based his probable cause for my *Warrant for Arrest* on the conversation from *The Sinister Telephone Call* chapter in a *sworn* affidavit. As you read Ghent's Affidavit, look with an eye toward detail and then refer back to the telephone conversation. It's amazing how SBI Ghent altered the substance of conversation by changing or adding a few words.

On September 11, 2006, Detective Simpson of the Brunswick County Sheriff's Office and Special Agent Ghent of the State Bureau of Investigation were shown various emails collaborating the victim's allegations on the suspect, Luke Stidham.

The victim, Brittany Lewis, logged into her MySpace account using the username of "your_little_playgirl_69_me@internet.com," and then showed Detective Simpson and myself numerous emails sent by a user identifying himself as "Luke." Detective Simpson then copied, printed, and recorded the email using forensic software.

I then instructed the victim to conduct a recorded telephone conversation between the victim and the suspect at which time, the suspect made several statements that also collaborate with the victim's allegations.

The suspect was asked if he was sure that his vasectomy worked. The suspect responded, "I'm 100% sure, why?" The victim was then told to say that she was pregnant by the suspect. The suspect replied, "That's not good." The suspect then replied, "You would not be pregnant by me, I've had a vasectomy."

The suspect made reference that someone was going to see by her phone bill that she had been calling him too much. The victim was instructed to ask, "They don't know about anything, right?' The suspect replied, "Right."

Copies of the emails are attached.

Based upon my training, experience, and investigation with this case, your Affiant, SBI Special Agent Ghent, seeks to charge the suspect, Luther Luke Stidham with one count of Statutory Rape (sexual penetration), one count of Statutory Sex Offense (digital penetration), and two counts of Indecent Liberties with a minor (Kissing for sexual gratification).

Upon being duly sworn, I declare under penalty of perjury that the foregoing is true and correct to the best of my knowledge.

Executed this 13th day of September 2006.

By: Special Agent Ghent of the State Bureau of Investigation.

•

In the *video recording* of this telephone conversation, Brittany, dressed in large clothing, sits at a small child's table. There was a chalkboard, wooden blocks, and crayons placed on and around the table. The camera was placed high in the air pointing down on Brittany, manipulating the appearance of a small child. Agent Ghent held up cue cards instructing Brittany on what to say.

Sherri, Lou, and Deputy Simpson sat at the table with Brittany. Agent Ghent sat beside Detective Simpson. "I need you to call Luke so I can record him." Agent Ghent said.

Brittany turned to her mother and then said, "They told me I wouldn't have to do this. If they keep messing with my head, I'm going to be the way I was before. I don't want to do this anymore."

"Has anyone else ever had sex with you or tried to have sex with you?" Deputy Simpson then asked.

"My brother tried to *force* me once." Brittany replied.

Sherri leaned next to Brittany and then whispered something in her ear. Deputy Simpson took notice.

Detective Simpson opened Ghent's case file and then took out emails that Brittany said I had sent her. After scanning several of the emails, Detective Simpson looked concerned about their content.

"Can someone gain access to a computer without the password?" Detective Simpson asked.

"Yeah, anyone can," Brittany said, as she perked up in her chair like she was a proud wanna-be hacker. Brittany then admitted that the computer belonged to her father.

Agent Ghent then left the room only to return moments later to briefly discuss something that he found on Brittany's computer:

"We found some embarrassing stuff on your computer." Ghent said.

"I know. My brother was supposed to delete it." Brittany responded.

"Don't worry about it." Ghent said. We'll take care of it."

•

You'll soon discover what SBI Agent Charles L. Ghent, FBI Agent Richard Novelli, Judge Ola May Lewis, Meredith Everhart, and Mike Ramos hid from the public in order to bolster their case against me and to protect Brittany Lewis and her creditability in Appendix B.

•

The remaining actions and conversation were as narrated in *The Sinister Telephone Call*. However, if you'll recall where Brittany suddenly shouted, "No" for no apparent reason, Agent Ghent was holding up a cue card instructing her to say that she was pregnant.

Within a few months of the recorded telephone call, and before Mike Ramos had joined the prosecution, Mike told me that Detective Simpson abruptly removed herself from the case, and then immediately resigned from the Brunswick County Sheriff's office.

"Why?" I asked him.

"She just up and left," he said. "No one knows where she's at."

Strangely, and unbeknownst to me, Detective Simpson's audio and video recording of her initial interview with Brittany on September 11, 2006 disappeared, and had it not been for the forthcoming *The Conspiracy Fax* subchapter, I never would have known.

The whereabouts of Detective Simpson's actual DVD recording of Brittany's interview are still unknown.

DANIELLE SHRUGGS

Before Danielle Shruggs's and Scott Cisco's were interviewed, and because they were friends of mine, we agreed to not discuss their conversation with the private investigator before my trial. That way no collaboration accusations could be made. And although I have included their statement in this section, I knew about the interview, but never read either one until on or about October 18, 2009. I thought this would be a great time to share what they had to say:

Danielle Shruggs currently resides at 101 Elm St., Boiling Spring Lakes, North Carolina with her boyfriend, Scott Cisco.

      Shruggs and her fiancé became interested in doing "ride-along" with police officers of the Boiling Spring Lakes Police Department in early 2006. Shruggs and her fiancé first went on a "ride along" with Officer Gene Dailey. Her fiancé knew Officer Dailey previously and they chose to begin doing the "ride along" with him. Her fiancé has known Officer Dailey for two or three years. Shruggs and her fiancé then met Officer Luke Stidham through Officer Dailey. Shruggs believes she first met Officer Stidham in December 2005 at a Boiling Spring Lakes Fire Department Christmas party. Shruggs and her fiancé mostly rode together with one of these two officers and rarely did Shruggs and her fiancé spilt up and ride separate from the other. She only rode with Officer Stidham on one occasion without her fiancé being present.

On one occasion, she went on a "ride-along" with Officer Stidham when his mobile telephone continuously rang. Officer Stidham would hit the "end" button and a short time later the phone would ring again. This continued on throughout the shift. Officer Stidham told Shruggs this was a 16-year-old girl who was just trying to get attention. Shruggs advised Officer Stidham was a very nice guy and would never want to hurt anyone's feelings. Shruggs observed Officer Stidham hand the telephone to Officer Dailey so that he did not have to talk with this young girl. On the time this happened, his mobile telephone rang at least twenty times during the shift. Shruggs normally would start the "ride along" around eight or nine p.m. and would head home around three a.m. Shruggs and her fiancé would normally be out on the "ride along" two or three times a week during July and August 2006.

Shruggs considers Luke Stidham and his wife to be friends of her and her fiancé. Shruggs and her fiancé helped Stidham do some work on their new home.

Shruggs was alone with Officer Stidham on only a few occasions other than the "ride-along." Officer Stidham never made any comments or talked about a relationship with any females regardless of age.

SCOTT CISCO

Cisco has been a volunteer fireman for the Boiling Spring Lakes Fire Department over the last four and a half years. He has not been able to participate in training or responding to fires due to job commitments. Cisco owns his own business in the construction and renovation trade. He also works as a wrecker service driver at night, and is on standby for callouts.

Cisco has known Officer Dailey of the Boiling Spring Lakes Police Department for a number of years. Approximately five to six months ago, Cisco and his fiancé began doing "ride-along" with Officer Dailey in the evenings and early hours of the morning. Cisco and his fiancé were spending two to three nights each week doing this. After a while, they began doing "ride-along" with Officer Stidham when Officer Dailey wasn't working on a particular night. Cisco first met Luke shortly after he began working at the police department. Cisco has socialized with Luke, and has been to his residence in Boiling Spring Lakes. Cisco considers himself to be friends with both Officer Dailey and Officer Stidham.

On one of his rides with Luke, his work mobile telephone rang more than fifty-five times between the hours of eight pm and two am. Luke did not answer any of the telephone calls throughout the evening, and continued to hang up on each incoming call. Luke told Cisco the telephone calls were from a girl he was trying to help. He further told Cisco this girl was having trouble with her mother.

Officer Dailey told Cisco that he and Luke were working together one evening approximately two weeks before Luke's arrest. The police mobile telephone rang, and Luke seen that it was an incoming call from Brittany. Luke handed the mobile telephone to Officer Dailey. Officer Dailey told Cisco that the girl said she had taken a bottle of pills. Both Officer Dailey and Luke went to the residence. Officer Dailey then said that the walls in her bedroom were covered with pictures of personnel of the Boiling Spring Lakes Police Department, and Fire Department along with department vehicles.

Cisco advised he has never observed Luke involved in any lengthy conversations with high school aged girls nor has he ever made any inappropriate comments about women. Cisco always considered Luke to be very professional in his demeanor and actions.

Cisco feels confident he was with Luke throughout the week when the statutory rape allegation occurred. During this particular week, Officer Dailey "had some things to take care of" and was not working any night shifts. During this time, both Cisco and his fiancé were with Luke most nights that he worked. Cisco stated that Danette said that Luke was with her during the hour of the night Brittany claimed she had sex with him.

●

The next six interviews and SBI Laboratory Report revealed several interesting issues, all of which seemed to have gone unchecked, or at least, ignored by the prosecution and my attorney.

JOHNNY T. LEWIS

On October 5, 2006, Agent Ghent interviewed Johnny T. Lewis, the father of the victim at an office in the Brunswick County Sheriff's Office. His report reflects that the following events occurred:

Johnny said he had no clue about Brittany's involvement with Officer Luke Stidham. He *signed* a release form about two or three days before Brittany went on a ride-along with Officer Stidham.

Brittany had told him that she was planning to do the ride-along, and Johnny told her to be back home at 9:30 p.m. Brittany walked in the door at 10:30 p.m. Johnny explained that Brittany told Luke that she had to be home by 10:30 p.m. instead.

Johnny said that he has a MySpace account that he started so that he could monitor what Brittany was doing Online. He said that he never noticed Stidham's messages on her page.

Johnny stated that he had deleted some pornographic images that he found on Brittany's computer. He saw that some of the pornographic images depicted *bestiality*, while others depicted Brittany *nude*. Johnny did this when Brittany was admitted to the hospital for the suicide attempt. Johnny said that his son must have deleted anything that was not deleted by him.

Johnny said that he never noticed anything being wrong with Brittany. On the night she attempted suicide, he saw that she was awake and on her computer. The next thing he knew, Stidham and another officer came to the door. They told

Johnny that Brittany had called 911 and said that she overdosed. The paramedics that arrived said that they did not think anything was wrong with her. At the hospital, Johnny learned that Brittany had probably taken eight Tylenol pills out of the bottle. Johnny stated that he thought that the entire attempt was just Brittany trying to get attention.

Johnny said that he had learned from his girlfriend, Donna Millowsky about a conversation she had with Stidham on the night Brittany was taken to the hospital. Stidham told Donna that Brittany had previously accused Johnny of molestation.

Johnny said that Donna had also found a letter that Brittany wrote to one of her friends saying that her father had raped her. Johnny never saw this letter. He first heard about it a couple of days after Brittany overdosed. Johnny believed that the letter was handwritten, and his girlfriend, Donna Millowsky, tore the letter up.

DONNA MILLOWSKY

Later that evening, Agent Ghent then interviewed Donna Millowsky. His report reflected that the following events took place:

Donna showed SA Ghent several pieces of a torn-up letter. Donna said that she found the letter in Brittany's closet on the day that she got home from Brynn Marr Hospital. Brittany was angry that she was going to go live with her mother and blamed Stidham for telling on her. Donna felt that Brittany had left the letter out, and that it was intended to be seen.

Donna said that on the night Brittany took the pills, the police officers showed up at around 2:30 a.m. It was Officer Stidham and Officer Dailey. Donna remembered that at one point, she was in the dining room smoking a cigarette, and talking to Stidham. At the same time, Johnny was in the back bedroom with the other officer and Brittany. Stidham said that Brittany told him that her mother was using drugs, and that her dad was abusive toward her. Donna said that in hindsight, she thinks that Brittany told Stidham those things to get his attention. She said that Brittany was a very smart girl, and that Brittany often uses her parent's against each other.

On the night that Brittany took the pills, Donna noticed a number of open programs on Brittany's computer task bar. When Donna returned home, only two were still up.

Donna said that she guessed Brittany's brother might have cleared some things off of her computer. He also was probably deleting some porn he had looked at, and his MySpace stuff. Donna said that he might have also believed that he was protecting Brittany by deleting things.

Donna provided Special Agent Charles L. Ghent with a poem that was handwritten by Brittany.

The poems read:

Daddy's little princess got into a fight. Mommy's little angel went under the knife. Another sad story of innocence gone by. But guess who's the one that's left to cry.

Daddy's little girl found out she's insane. Mommy's little baby's hooked on cocaine. In fifteen minutes she'll be out getting laid. Just so she can get her night's pay. Daddy's little love is popping some pills.

Mommy's little sweet pea is skipping her meals. Gotta be thin to get your thrills. She'll never get her fill. Daddy's little hunny's writing her story in pen. Mommy's little darling has a gun to her head. The trigger is pulled, another child is dead. I guess that's one less mouth to be fed.

What if today is the day I die? Would you come to my funeral? Would you even cry? Would you look at the sky and ask why? How would you say your good bye? **Would you forgive me if I ever told a lie? This is what goes through my head, every night before I go to bed.**

How do you feel, when you watch your prey? When you see them cower in fear? And shrink away from you. How do you feel, when you pin them down? When you see their terror? And you feel there panic? How do you feel, when you smother them? When you roughly kiss them? And your hands start to wander. How do you feel, when you watch them cry? When you rape them violently? And force them to give. How do you feel? Or do you feel at all? How did you feel when you raped me last night?

SBI DNA LABORATORY REPORT

As I present the next document, I'll note that it was delivered to Special Agent Charles L. Ghent just a few days prior to his "Synopsis" report. I believe that this report would have played a crucial role in my defense, hence why the judicial tag-team collaborated to withhold it from my knowledge. You're the jury here, remember? You be the judge.

On October 13, 2006 SBI Forensic Biologist, Ruben A. Harley, conducted an examination for semen from several items recovered from the back of my patrol vehicle from the night of my arrest (September 11, 2006).

His report reflected that the following items were analyzed:

Unlike F.B.I. Agent Richard Novelli's laboratory report that was presented into evidence by Special Agent Charles L. Ghent, S.B.I. Agent Harley certified his analysis above with his signature to be "true and accurate."

CHIEF RICHARD WHITE

Special Agent Charles L. Ghent interviewed Chief Richard White on Wednesday, October 18, 2006. The interview was conducted in Chief White's office at the Boiling Spring Lakes Police Department.

Chief White stated that Luke Stidham was hired at the BSL Police Department May 02, 2005, as a traffic officer. After several months of training, he was promoted to the Governor's Highway Safety Program Traffic (GHSP) Officer's position. White stated that Stidham's salary was 100% funded by grants. White stated that Stidham was responsible for those grants and where the funds were dispersed.

White stated that Stidham was a mediocre officer and that if he had not been the GHSP Officer, he would have fired him. He said that Stidham had caused him problems in the past by failing to perform his duties correctly.

White said that Stidham often had several females of unknown ages calling the police department asking for him. White also stated that many of these females that were local to BSL, would stop by the police department looking for him.

White said that he thought Stidham had been having an affair with a married female by the name of Michelle because she would stop by the police department a lot asking when he was coming on duty.

White said that he never gave Stidham permission to give Brittany a ride-along in the BSL patrol vehicle. White also stated that he did not sign any approval form. White stated that he thought Stidham was trying to cover up for himself.

•

Conveniently, Special Agent Charles L. Ghent omitted to report on a telephone conversation he conducted with Michelle about the alleged affair introduced by Chief White.

A few weeks after the chief's interview, I ran into Michelle and Kevin Young in Boiling Spring Lakes. Michelle told me that Special Agent Charles L. Ghent telephoned her about the alleged affair.

Michelle stated that she told Ghent that she and her husband helped me in the construction of my house. Michelle said that she and I never had an affair, (and we didn't) nor did I make any advancements toward her. Michelle told Ghent that Officer Dailey and Chief White started the rumor because I had let their children go on a ride-along. Michelle then told Ghent that Officer Dailey and Chief White had harassed her in the past.

Michelle added that she and her husband were friends of mine. She then said, "Luke, just liked to help other people."

CLARA MILLINGS

Interview conducted by Agent Ghent in the South Brunswick Middle School's Principal's Office. Agent Ghent's report reflected that the following events took place:

Millings said that she first met Stidham sometime after July 16, 2006, when she returned from Bristol, Tennessee. Milling's friend Jee Holton, had come down from Bristol to visit during that time.

Millings stated that when they got to Kopp's Quik Stop, Stidham was already there with his patrol SUV. Millings said that Stidham was always on duty when she saw him. Brittany went up to Stidham and talked to him. She then introduced Stidham to Millings and Holton.

Millings said that they saw Stidham near the park two or three times. The police department and park share the same parking lot. They walked to the park a lot during the summer and not always because Stidham was there, but Brittany would always say that he was going to be there on the times that they saw him. She said that Brittany and Stidham usually did not say too much and just made small talk.

Millings said that Holton, Brittany, and she walked to the stop sign on the road where Brittany lived. Millings said that she knew it was a planned meeting between Stidham and Brittany because Brittany had said that. The three girls walked out of the front door sometime between 11 p.m. and midnight and went to the stop sign. Shortly after they got to the stop sign, Stidham pulled up in his patrol SUV.

Brittany went over and briefly talked to him at the window. Holton and Millings stood back for a little bit while they talked, and Millings said she could not remember what they talked about. Millings and Holton got into the SUV after about two minutes of talking. Brittany got in the front seat.

Milling said that Stidham drove them around for a while, and then dropped them off back near Brittany's house.

Millings said that they saw Stidham a few other times at the store or at the parking lot of the police station. There were no other prearranged meetings.

Millings said that she never talked to her about any physical contact that she had with Stidham. Millings said that she thought it was weird, like the kind of crush that kids have on their teachers.

Millings said that a week before this interview, Brittany pulled her into the corner and told her "I had sex with Luke," but said that she had been trying to hide it because Brittany was a friend.

Millings then admitted that the only comment that she could recall posting in Stidham's MySpace account was on the night of the ride-along. She posted "Interesting." and Jee posted, "Interesting." Brittany then posted, "Yeah that was interesting." Millings said that they were posted in Stidham's MySpace account. However, Millings stated that after Brittany logged out of her account, she later noticed that Brittany's comment appeared to be changed.

BOBBY MCCORKLE

Agent Ghent conducted an interview with Bobby McCorkle by telephone. Agent Ghent's report reflects the following events took place.

McCorkle was interviewed as to his knowledge of Brittany Lewis, Luke Stidham, and Larry "Buddy" Gysel. McCorkle is the ex-boyfriend of Brittany.

McCorkle stated that he dated Brittany for approximately seven months, beginning shortly after his 17th birthday. He said that he knew Buddy from church.

McCorkle said that he once *recorded* Brittany accusing someone of trying to rape her. She has accused McCorkle of hitting her in the past, and she accused a guy named Bryan of sexual harassment. McCorkle stated that Brittany couldn't be trusted.

McCorkle said that he caught Brittany cheating on him with Buddy. On that day, he called her house, and Brittany's brother told McCorkle that Brittany had gone jogging. McCorkle was suspicious, so he drove down her road.

McCorkle stated that as he pulled onto the road, he could see her running beside Buddy's truck. McCorkle said that he pulled up beside Brittany and started yelling at her. She got in his vehicle, and they drove the rest of the way to her house. Back at the house, the two continued fighting about what had just happened. Brittany told McCorkle that she and Buddy did not do anything. Brittany then admitted to McCorkle that Buddy stuck his finger in her vagina. Brittany then finally admitted to McCorkle that she and Buddy had sex.

McCorkle asked Brittany if she had been talking to Buddy on the computer, which he suspected because he saw Buddy's name on some instant messages. Brittany pulled up one of the instant messages and showed it to McCorkle. McCorkle said that the message was very graphic. He could not remember everything on it, but he recalled a line that read, "Bobby's penis is real small."

McCorkle said that Officer Stidham pulled him over one day, along with another Boiling Spring Lakes officer. Stidham told McCorkle that he pulled him over for street racing, where he was issued a citation. McCorkle said that he knew that Stidham was friends with Buddy, and he believed that Buddy may have asked Stidham to pull him over.

McCorkle said that he believes that Brittany and Stidham had sex. He said that Brittany originally told him that she was sixteen. McCorkle said that as he got to know Brittany, he realized that she could not be trusted.

JEE L. HOLTON

Special Agent Charles L. Ghent interviewed Holton on Wednesday, October 18, 2006, beginning at approximately 3:04 p.m. The interview was conducted by telephone:

Holton stated that she met Stidham approximately two or three days before she went on a ride-along in his police vehicle. Holton said that one day, Brittany and Millings wanted her to meet Stidham, so they all walked to the park behind the Boiling Spring Lakes Police Department. Holton stated that Luke seemed like a big brother.

Two or three days after meeting Stidham, Holton spent the night at Brittany's house. Brittany told Millings and Holton that they were all going to sneak out and go on a ride-along with Stidham.

Holton said that Stidham met them near Brittany's house in his patrol vehicle. Millings and Holton got in the back, and Brittany got in the front seat. Holton said that Stidham drove them to check on the school and did his usual routine.

Holton said that she had a MySpace account. Holton added Stidham as a friend on the day that they met. She had seen him on Brittany and Milling's friend list. Holton said that this was not unusual.

Holton said that she did not see Brittany and Stidham kiss, and she didn't know why Brittany would have said that she and Millings stood watching. Holton then said that Brittany had told her and Millings that she thought Stidham was really cute.

SPECIAL AGENT GHENT'S SYNOPSIS

Just four days upon the conclusion of Jee Holton's interview, Agent Ghent prepared his case report by modifying his *Warrant for Arrest* Affidavit. He added six paragraphs; the second, third, fourth, and last paragraphs would have been vital to my defense.

Brittany stated that in July of 2006, she went on a ride-along with Officer Stidham. This was an official ride-along that was *approved* by Brittany's father, Johnny T. Lewis, and Chief White.

On or about July 25, 2006 she snuck out of her house for a second ride-along and brought along her friends Clara Millings and Jee Holton.

Brittany stated that on this ride-along, she did kiss Stidham and that Jee Holton and Clara Millings stood watching the entire event. Clara and Jee confirmed that the ride-along occurred; although, *neither* said that they actually witnessed the kiss.

Brittany went on a third ride-along, and she said that she gave Stidham a "pop-kiss" on the cheek.

Brittany and Stidham then met for a forth ride-along on or about August 22, 2006, and that on that ride-along, the two of them had sexual intercourse on the backseat of the patrol vehicle. Brittany said that Stidham again kissed her, inserted a finger in her vagina, and did not use a condom during this incident.

Brittany stated that she had saved all or most of the messages from Stidham prior to being admitted by him to Brynn Marr Hospital. Brittany provided

investigators with the account details and login information for her MySpace®
account. Investigators then changed her login information so that only the
investigators had access.

●

The date at which the emails were actually printed (September 11, 2006) was
recorded on each page of the emails. Special Agent Charles L. Ghent then produced
additional emails that were even more incriminating. The printed date recorded by
the new emails was September 13, 2006; two days after Brittany Lewis no longer had
access.

As you'll recall during the interrogation, Ghent returned with a laptop that I
naively used to login my email account with.

I later discovered from Charles L. Ghent's own report, that before he had
returned with the laptop, he secretly activated a "keystroke logger devise" to record
my user-name and password *without* court authorization or my permission; both a
State Felony and Federal criminal offense under the Electronic Communications
Privacy Act.

It bothered me immensely for years that Charles L. Ghent had complete
control of my email account. Looking back, maybe that solved the riddle of who
mysteriously deleted my email account just days after the interrogation, as well as
explained all the *copy and paste* errors on several pages of the evidentiary emails. I was
still in the Brunswick County jail.

According to a cover letter typed by Special Agent Ghent, on January 7,
2007, he met with FBI Special Agent Richard Novelli for the purpose of reviewing

the results of a Hyper Text Markup Language (html) forensic examination conducted on a computer hard drive recovered from Brittany's home.

I found it strange that there was no official FBI analysis or certified report attached to the examination.

Other than Ghent's cover letter, there was no record that anyone from the FBI even conducted the examination in the first place, although FBI policy requires it. Ghent's cover letter was stapled to the front of the forensic examination, which were several pages of html code.

When considering all the scams the SBI had gotten themselves caught up in lately, and after reviewing the code thoroughly, it then became clear why an actual FBI case report was missing.

The html code recovered from the documentary record was reconstructed by adding the few missing lines of code to properly construct a working web page. Upon activating the html file, it attempted to log back into my now *deleted* email account.

After a closer inspection of the code, the proof was in the pudding from the onset. Two single lines of code revealed that Brittany's computer recorded itself logged into my email account viewing her own profile.

The first line read, "InboxtoUserId=7765472."

If we break this code down, here is how it will read:

The email's "Inbox" belongs to User ID number 7765472.

User Id number 7765472 was assigned to me by MySpace under my user name "Luke".

The second line read, "viewfriendprofiletoUserId=6084xxxx." (User Id redacted).

If we break down this code, it translates to read:

This person was "viewing" the "friend profile" of User ID number 608xxxx.

Guess whom that user Id belonged to?

It's called Phishing!

CONSPIRACY FAX

As I read over all the above documents, angry tears filled my eyes, and I thought, *Why did you strip me of such?*" I then stumbled upon this fax that left me both breathless and boiling with rage.

As you read the prosecutor's fax, note its date and then refer back to my trial day. Be very attentive to *"detail."*

```
Brunswick County
District Attorney
Bolivia, NC 28422
(910) 555-2852


August 28, 2008.


Dear Mike,

Here are the details you requested per our
meeting. Also, as I stated on the telephone, I
wanted to give you notice of some motions that
I will be filing this week, and then asking to
be heard on at trial. Please let me know if you
think any of them need to be heard ahead of
time, and if necessary, we can find a judge in
civil court this week:

    1. Rule 412 Motion - I will be filing a
standard Rule 412 Motion, but I will also be
asking specifically that nothing is mentioned
regarding any sexual activity with or charges
resulting from sexual activity with Buddy.
```

2. Motion in Limine - Mistake of Fact - I will be filing a motion to prevent any mention of a possible mistake of fact with regard to Brittany's age.

3. Motion in Limine - *Prior or Subsequent False Allegations* - There are several mention in the discovery provided by the *State* to *you* that contains several *third-party* hearsay statements that, if believed, would tend to indicate that the victim has previously made accusations of prior physical and sexual abuse against several individuals, including a prior *boyfriend* and her own *father*. We have no reason to believe that the victim ever made such accusations.

In addition to these Motions, I also wanted to let you know that I *spoke* with Richard Novelli from the FBI *again* this afternoon. He does actually have the computers from Luke's patrol SUV and the computer from the BSL PD. He never did a report on them, but he *is* going to get me a *report* by *tomorrow* on what is on both of those. From speaking with him, they both show that Stidham was going to MySpace on those computers. I don't know if he was able to retrieve any emails, but if he did, *I will pass them on to you tomorrow*.

Finally, I want to let you know that I have someone from the Sheriff's Department trying to locate any additional information that they might have retained in Detective Simpson's file when she *left* regarding this case, including a copy of the victim's interview, both the *recording* and *transcript*. They are supposed to let me know by tomorrow if they have anything. In the meantime, I would appreciate it if you could have your office fax me a *copy* of the transcript that you have of the victim's interview with Simpson. I *don't* have that for some reason.

Thanks, and please let me know if *you* think that there is anything else *missing*.

Sincerely Yours,

Meredith Everhart

Assistant District Attorney

Someone Who Has Nothing to Hide Hides Nothing!

The prosecutor's testimony at my trial was belied by her own fax. I also found it insulting that she was extremely comfortable asking my attorney to replace *any* evidence that he thought had also disappeared when Detective Simpson left regarding the case. I felt like that was like an enormous slap to the face.

Despite her fax, Ms. Everhart's statement at my trial hearing was so connected with the fact directly at issue as to have a legitimate tendency to prove that no full forensics was actually *requested* or *done* on my two computers.

Meredith Everhart had requested this forensics herself!

So why the need to lie about the forensics? And when I think about it even today that Mike Ramos stood there saying nothing, burned my ass something fierce.

"You mother trucking sum mama beach." I often said. It seemed to go without saying that had the results of FBI Special Agent Richard Novelli's forensics been damaging to my defense, surely Meredith would have presented that to the trial court instead of denying it existed. It made me wonder what else she was hiding.

Next, define *third-party* hearsay and then refer back to Bobby McCorkle and Johnny Lewis's interview and then to Brittany's statement in the *video recording* of *The Sinister Telephone Call* in this Appendix. What you'll find was not all *third-party* hearsay.

And last but not least, you may be interested to know that the whereabouts of FBI Special Agent Richard Novelli's forensics that Meredith's denied existed during my trial are also unknown.

The next section may offer some explanation as to why Ms. Everhart felt it imperative to avoid a comparison forensics by an outside computer expert—at any cost.

●

Is it just and fair when the justice system turns a blind eye to their alleged victim's possession of child pornography and other illegal images in order to secure a foul conviction against a suspect?

The Lewis's family computer operated on Windows 98 Second Edition. It contained two IDE Hard Drives; labeled as "C" and "D" drive, and one CD ROM; labeled as "E" drive. Both the computers seized from the BSL Police Department operated on Windows XP Professional Edition. And as for my son's computer? —Windows 95. All of which had only one IDE Hard Drive; labeled as "C" drive, and one CD ROM; labeled as "D" drive.

After an adamant proclamation of my innocence, I contacted the FBI Headquarters about the images. The child pornography possession allegations against me were immediately retracted.

A hand-written note was discovered taped to the backside of one of the many suppressed interviews in my case file. The note indicated that Mike Ramos had already informed the prosecutor that the illegal images were recovered from a computer that Johnny, JR, and Brittany all shared.

As you'll recall, Special Agent Charles L. Ghent seized Brittany's computer after her stepmother and own father informed him that they had found the illegal images on her computer. Agent Ghent then informed Brittany that he had found some "embarrassing stuff on her computer" during *The Sinister Telephone Call* chapter. The "embarrassing stuff" were actual pornographic images of Brittany.

The fact that a 14-year-old Brittany took pornographic pictures of herself and then stored them on her father's computer does not exempt her from the law.

Although at least four members of the prosecutor's tag-team knew where those images were recovered from, not one person in the Lewis family was charged with possession of child pornography. Not one.

The discovery of the illegal images on Brittany's computer was withheld from the media and the public--until now.

Senior Resident Superior Court Judge Ola May Lewis, despite her own recusal, has knowingly and willingly interfered into my appeal process.

Without authority and while defying her requirement to remain impartial, Judge Lewis denied my first Motion for Appropriate Relief, and then has refused to allow *ANY* other court to address any further motions or writs filed by me.

In 2010, while in prison, I filed a Notice of Appeal with the Brunswick County Superior Court, challenging the trial courts authority since it is on record that I refused to sign the Second Degree Rape *Bill of Information.*

According to the NC Court of Appeal Rules and Regulations, the Superior Court Clerk of Court is to then forward the Notice of Appeal to the Appellate Court without delay.

Judge Ola May Lewis then immediately intercepted my Notice of Appeal and refused to allow it to be forwarded to the NC Court of Appeal.

In late summer of 2011, I asked my wife, Danette to contact Judge Lewis for an update on the Notice of Appeal since we had not received word of a court appointed attorney. Danette was redirected to Judge Lewis's voicemail where she left a detailed message.

Judge Ola Lewis had her secretary, Tammy Pierce return Danette's telephone call. Tammy Pierce then left a voicemail message stating:

"Judge Ola Lewis has barred Luther Stidham from any further motions, writs or petitions and the court will not address these issues."

APPENDIX B:

THE AFTERMATH

Brittany Lewis remained at the Brynn Marr Hospital undergoing mental evaluation for approximately two weeks. She never once accused me of being the reason for the suicide attempt. The doctor's report revealed that Brittany named Buddy, Johnny, Lou, and her mother as the reasons for the suicide attempt. I later read in the transcript of her interview with Detective Simpson that she told the doctors what they wanted to hear so they would let her go home.

Beginning in 2009, I filed numerous complaints against Special Agent Charles L. Ghent and the prosecutor with both the state's Attorney General and The NC State Bureau of Investigation. On the notion that no one is above the law, I repeatedly requested that they be charged with Perjury and Obstruction of Justice. Neither office cared enough to even respond. Special Agent Charles L. Ghent has since resigned from his position. He moved back to his hometown, Mt. Pleasant, South Carolina, and now is a special agent for S.L.E.D.

Judge Gary Locklear sentenced me to serve 54 months minimum to 74 months maximum behind bars for the second-degree rape conviction. He then added two, 13 to 16 month sentences for the taking indecent liberties with a minor convictions, but suspended both on terms of probation for a period of 36 months.

Thirty days after I was arrested, Buddy Gysel, charged with the same crimes, fled to Philadelphia avoiding arrest. His attorneys negotiated a plea deal in exchange for his return -- 30 days in the Brunswick County Jail and three years' probation. Although Buddy admitted to sexual intercourse with Brittany over a three-year period, he plead guilty to one count of taking indecent liberties with a child. Ms. Everhart dismissed all other charges.

Despite numerous protests, Chief Richard White became BSL's mayor. Even today, along the roadside of Hwy 87 one can find the occasional posted protesting signs: "*White Liar!*"

In February 2012, Mayor White terminated Lt. Ledbetter for campaigning against him. It is rumored that the termination came swiftly after he refused to participate in White's upcoming electoral campaign. A reliable informant at the BSL Police Department referred to White's election as "rigged." He went on to state that Mayor White is "playing for votes, and has his own agenda that doesn't benefit BSL"

In September 2012, Mayor Richard White turned himself over to police after learning that a *Warrant* had been issued for his arrest for Sexual Battery. Within weeks, a second female came forward with the same accusation. After some digging into his background, it was then discovered that this wasn't the first time Richard

White had been charged with Sexual Battery. He had faced the same charge at least once before in 2000, where he eventually settled out of court avoiding prosecution.

Richard White has denied any wrongdoing, and as of the date that I wrote this book, his trial was still pending.

So, (you know I can't resist) if Richard White was truly innocent, now he knows what it feels like to be *Falsely Accused*, and unless his victims recant their allegation, *Forever Branded*.

●

While here in prison, I received word from Mrs. Bailey's family that she had passed away. Her son wrote and said that she kept clippings of my arrest and an article about me from the *Stateport Pilot* in Southport. "She spoke of you often." He wrote. "I know she missed you."

I thought this would be the perfect opportunity for me to pay my respects from behind these bars so I included this small tribute:

Dear Mrs. Bailey,
Good-bye my old friend. You will forever hold a special memory in my heart.
Your Friend,
Eleven Seventy-Seven

ABOUT THE AUTHOR

After his release from prison, Luke's plans included starting a website based on his pursuit of innocence, and although the odds are stacked against him, to continue raising funds to overturn his conviction. He says,

"Never give up, right? It is my goal to become the protestant against unfair trial practices, who is dedicated to protecting human rights. It is also my hope to establish a forum to influence unity and equality among all people."

The variety of odd jobs he has held, moving to many residences, and aborted careers is due more to the fact that Luke Stidham had no direction in life. Raised by his mother, Luke grew up without a father's guidance and, in 1987, got himself kicked out of Ranson Junior High School. Thirteen years later, he obtained his GED.

A Charlotte, NC native, Luke became the typical 18-year-old long hair wanna-be rock and roll star. He and Bones, the drummer, formed a rock band that performed in a small bar north of Charlotte.

From flipping burgers, to scrubbing toilets, managing a pizza restaurant, being an auto mechanic, and working as a bartender, to selling prehistoric satellite dishes door-to-door, Luke was a jack-of-all-trades. He says, "I've even sold replacement windows."

Finally, at the age of 34, he pursued a childhood dream. He became a law enforcement officer. He said, when that dream came true, "One of my greatest blessings is that I enjoy helping people. It gives me an indescribable sense of personal satisfaction that those of us who carry this gift, are able to feel. As a police officer, I got that chance every day."

●

Having been sentenced to serve four-and-a-half years in prison, Luke explored a world he didn't know existed.

"I've learned many things and discovered a broken system."

Mentored by another inmate in his prison dorm, Luke excelled at drawing portraits. He volunteered his free time as a GED tutor for nearly 3 years. Luke has also studied law and kept a journal of his life in prison. As a jailhouse lawyer, he helped free the over-sentenced and won new trials for other inmates. As a convict, he earned the reputation as a marriage counselor, mediator, mentor, and tax preparer.

Now at age 46, Luke has dedicated himself to protecting human rights. Inspired by his cellmates, he writes about his experiences as a police officer and as a convict, and he shares his view on fundamental fairness.

"I found healing in writing. It's not a metaphor; it really works."

His writing experience includes a published grant proposal tutorial, several non-published legal research documents, and criminal incident reports. Often, his police reports were chosen to be published in local newspapers.

"I would love for you to share your own stories about your personal experience with the justice or prison system.

Email them to me at ldstidham885@gmail.com.

www.ingramcontent.com/pod-product-compliance
Lightning Source LLC
Chambersburg PA
CBHW032043040426
42334CB00038B/389